# Debbie Mumm's®

# FLORAL INSPIRATIONS

*A bright splash of tulips and playful pansies in a row,*
*The quiet serenity of a trellis and the delicacy of a garden mum,*
*Bring the outdoors inside and quilting inspiration to your home!*

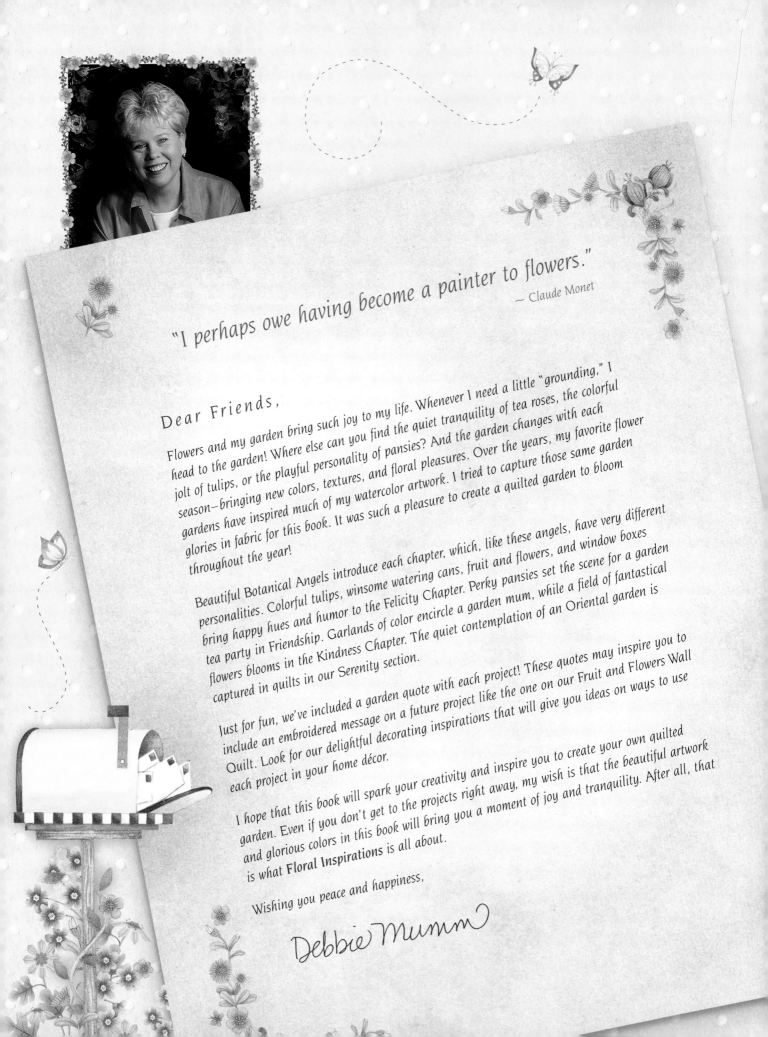

*"I perhaps owe having become a painter to flowers."*
~ Claude Monet

Dear Friends,

Flowers and my garden bring such joy to my life. Whenever I need a little "grounding," I head to the garden! Where else can you find the quiet tranquility of tea roses, the colorful jolt of tulips, or the playful personality of pansies? And the garden changes with each season—bringing new colors, textures, and floral pleasures. Over the years, my favorite flower gardens have inspired much of my watercolor artwork. I tried to capture those same garden glories in fabric for this book. It was such a pleasure to create a quilted garden to bloom throughout the year!

Beautiful Botanical Angels introduce each chapter, which, like these angels, have very different personalities. Colorful tulips, winsome watering cans, fruit and flowers, and window boxes bring happy hues and humor to the Felicity Chapter. Perky pansies set the scene for a garden tea party in Friendship. Garlands of color encircle a garden mum, while a field of fantastical flowers blooms in the Kindness Chapter. The quiet contemplation of an Oriental garden is captured in quilts in our Serenity section.

Just for fun, we've included a garden quote with each project! These quotes may inspire you to include an embroidered message on a future project like the one on our Fruit and Flowers Wall Quilt. Look for our delightful decorating inspirations that will give you ideas on ways to use each project in your home décor.

I hope that this book will spark your creativity and inspire you to create your own quilted garden. Even if you don't get to the projects right away, my wish is that the beautiful artwork and glorious colors in this book will bring you a moment of joy and tranquility. After all, that is what **Floral Inspirations** is all about.

Wishing you peace and happiness,

*Debbie Mumm*

# TABLE OF CONTENTS

## Felicity

## Friendship

## Kindness

## Serenity

# FELICITY

"*Earth laughs in flowers.*"

— Ralph Waldo Emerson

A bright splash of color as
tulips reach for the sky,
The delicacy of strawberry vines
stretching across the rich earth,
The soft shower of water
from a bright watering can,
The garden leaps to life with
the joy of spring's rebirth.

> "Just living is not enough," said the butterfly. "One must have sunshine, freedom, and a little flower."
>
> — Hans Christian Andersen

# Make your bedroom bloom!

Your bedroom will bloom with glorious color! Accent your quilt with a set of pillow shams (page 11) and an accent pillow using a single tulip block with colored borders. A small round table next to the bed can be draped with a circular cloth in a soft color and then accented with a bright colored square. We loved the idea of adding Prairie Points to the square topper to repeat the triangular motif of the tulips. A piece of an old picket fence, a trellis, or a wrought iron gate would make a wonderful headboard. Complete your garden theme with gardening accessories such as our painted window box.

# TULIP PATCH
## Bed Quilt

**Tulip Patch Bed Quilt**
*Finished size 87" x 97"*
*Photo page 9*

*Crisp Double Four-Patch Blocks mark an orderly path through this colorful fabric garden—just brimming with perky, paper-pieced tulips. This generously sized quilt assembles quickly, leaving lots of time to "smell the flowers."*

# Fabric Requirements and Cutting Instructions

Read all instructions before beginning and use $1/4$"-wide seam allowances throughout. Read Cutting the Strips and Pieces on page 78 prior to cutting fabrics.

| | First Cut | | Second Cut | |
| --- | --- | --- | --- | --- |
| | Number of Strips or Pieces | Dimensions | Number of Pieces | Dimensions |
| Fabric A Four-Patch *3" strips equal to 1 yard* | 20 | 3" x 21" | | |
| Fabric B Background *4 1/2 yards* | 12 | 4 1/2" x 42" | 56 | 4 1/2" x 6 3/4"* |
| | 5 | 3 1/2" x 42" | 56 | 3 1/2" x 3"* |
| | 27 | 3" x 42" | 20 | 3" x 21" |
| | | | 56 | 3" x 5 1/4" |
| | | | 112 | 3" squares *\*suggested size cuts for foundation paper-piecing* |
| Fabric C Blocks *1 1/3 yards* | 8 | 5 1/2" x 42" | 56 | 5 1/2" squares |
| Fabric D Leaves & Stems *1/2 yard each of two different greens* | 8 | 3" x 42" | 56 | 3" x 5 1/4" |
| | 4 | 1" x 42" | 28 | 1" x 5 1/2" |
| Fabric E Flower Centers *scraps* | 28 | 2 1/2" squares* | | *\*suggested size cuts for foundation paper-piecing* |
| Fabric F Flowers *1/4 yard each of seven different fabrics* *Each 1/4 yard will make four flowers.* | 1 | 4" x 42" | 4 | 4" x 7 1/2"* |
| | 1 | 3 1/2" x 42" *Cut for each fabric* | 4 | 3 1/2" x 5"* *\*suggested size cuts for foundation paper-piecing* |
| **Borders** | | | | |
| First Border *1/2 yard* | 8 | 1 1/2" x 42" | | |
| Second Border *1/3 yard* | 8 | 1" x 42" | | |
| Third Border *5/8 yard* | 9 | 2" x 42" | | |
| Outside Border *1 1/2 yards* | 9 | 5 1/2" x 42" | | |
| Binding *7/8 yard* | 10 | 2 3/4" x 42" | | |
| Backing - 8 yards Batting - 94" x 104" | | | | |

# Making the Blocks

You will be making 28 Double Four-Patch Blocks and 28 Flower Blocks. Finished size for both blocks is 10". The top half of each Flower Block is pieced over a paper foundation.

## Double Four-Patch Blocks

**1.** Sew 3" x 21" Fabric A strips and 3" x 21" Fabric B strips together in pairs to make twenty 5 1/2" x 21" strip sets. Press. Using rotary cutter and ruler, cut a total of one hundred twelve 3" segments (in matching pairs) from strip sets.

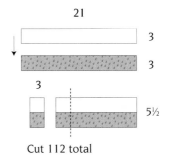

Cut 112 total

**2.** Arrange and sew segments in pairs as shown to make fifty-six units. Press.

Make 56

**3.** Sew each unit from step 2 to one 5 1/2" Fabric C square. Press. Make fifty-six.

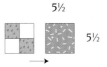

Make 56

**4.** Arrange and sew units from step 3 in pairs as shown. Press. Make twenty-eight. Block measures 10 1/2" x 10 1/2".

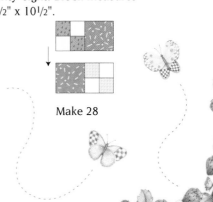

Make 28

## Flower Blocks

**1.** Refer to Quick Corner Triangle directions on page 78. Sew two 3" Fabric B squares to opposite corners of a 3" x 5¼" Fabric D piece as shown. Press. Make twenty-eight.

B = 3 x 3
D = 3 x 5¼          B = 3 x 3          Make 28

**2.** Repeat step 1 to sew two 3" Fabric B squares to opposite corners of each remaining 3" x 5¼" Fabric D piece as shown. Press. Make twenty-eight.

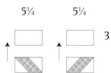

B = 3 x 3
D = 3 x 5¼          B = 3 x 3          Make 28

**3.** Sew one 3" x 5¼" Fabric B piece to each unit from step 1 and step 2 as shown. Press. Make twenty-eight of each.

5¼          5¼

3

Make 28 each

**4.** Sew one 1" x 5½" Fabric D strip between one of each unit from step 3. Press. Make twenty-eight.

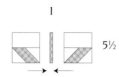

1

5½

**5.** Make at least twenty-eight copies of paper-piecing pattern on page 10. Make all copies from the same copier at the same time to avoid distortions.

**6.** Pin one 2½" Fabric E square right side up on blank side of a paper-piecing pattern, centering it over the area labeled 1. Be sure to cover entire area, allowing for ¼" seam allowance on all sides.

Right side
of fabric                          Unmarked
                                   side of
                                   pattern
E = 2½ x 2½
Dotted lines
indicate reverse (blank)
side of paper

**7.** Place one 3½" x 3" Fabric B piece right sides together with Fabric E piece, aligning raw edges. Pin away from seam line. **Flip paper pattern so printed side faces you. Stitch directly on printed line between areas 1 and 2 as shown.** Turn over pattern; fold back Fabric B piece and finger press. Make sure Fabric B piece completely covers area 2, allowing for ¼" seam allowance on all sides. Trim excess fabric ¼" away from stitch line.

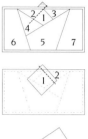

B = 3½ x 3

**8.** Repeat step 7 to add one 3½" x 3" Fabric B piece to opposite side of Fabric E piece as shown. Fold back to cover area 3, finger press, and trim seam.

B = 3½ x 3

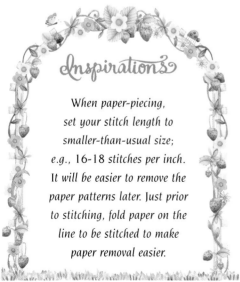

*Inspirations*

When paper-piecing,
set your stitch length to
smaller-than-usual size;
e.g., 16-18 stitches per inch.
It will be easier to remove the
paper patterns later. Just prior
to stitching, fold paper on the
line to be stitched to make
paper removal easier.

**10.** Repeat steps 7 and 8 to pin, stitch, flip, press, and trim 4½" x 6¾" Fabric B strips to paper-pieced block as shown, covering areas 6 and 7.

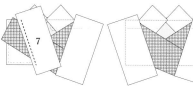

B = 4½ x 6¾

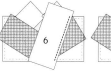

B = 4½ x 6¾

**11.** Using paper pattern for guidance, trim block to 10½" x 5½".

10½

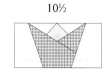

5½

Trim to 10½ x 5½

**12.** Repeat steps 6 through 11 to make total of 28 paper-pieced blocks.

**13.** Sew units from step 4 and step 12 together in pairs. Press seams toward leaf unit. Make twenty-eight blocks.

**9.** Repeat steps 7 and 8 to pin, stitch, flip, press, and trim seams matching 3½" x 5" and 4" x 7½" Fabric F pieces to paper-pieced block as shown. The 3½" x 5" piece covers area 4, and the 4" x 7½" piece covers area 5.

F = 3½ x 5

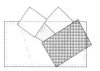

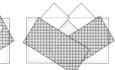

F = 4 x 7½

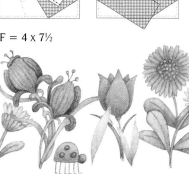

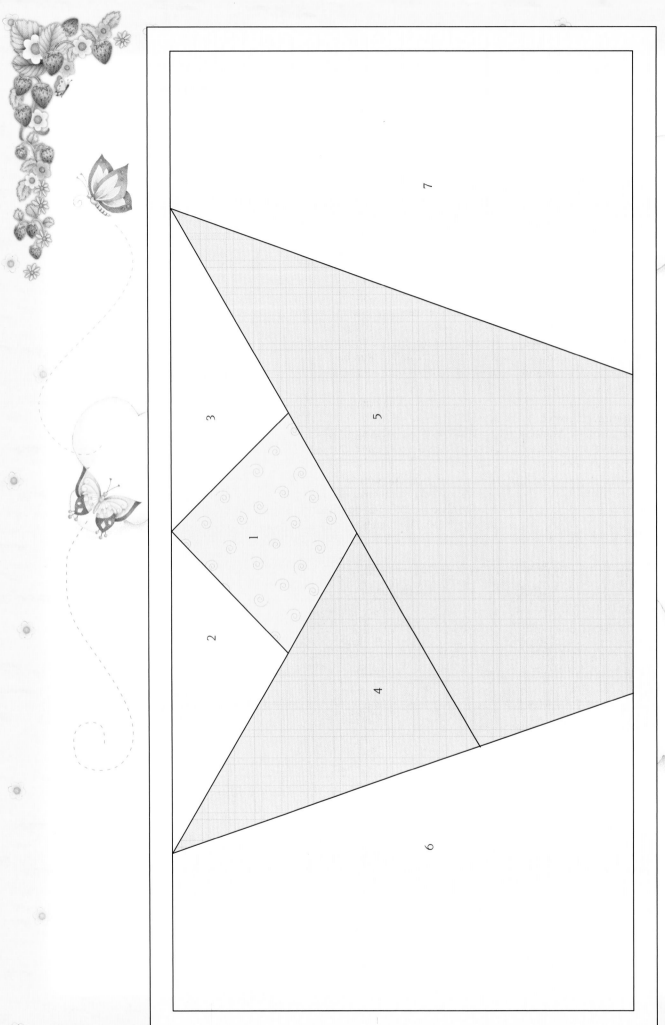

Permission to photocopy this page (page 10) is granted by Debbie Mumm, Inc. to aid in completion of the Tulip Patch Bed Quilt. Compare photocopy to original to make sure size is an accurate 10½" x 5½".

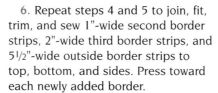

## Assembly

1. Refer to quilt layout on page 6. Arrange blocks in eight horizontal rows of seven blocks each, alternating Double Four-Patch and Flower Blocks in each row. Rows 1, 3, 5, and 7 begin with a Double Four-Patch Block, while Rows 2, 4, 6, and 8 begin with a Flower block.

2. Sew blocks together into rows. Press seams in opposite directions from row to row.

3. Sew rows together. Press.

4. Sew 1¹/₂" x 42" first border strips end to end to make one continuous 1¹/₂"-wide strip. Measure quilt through center from side to side. Cut two 1¹/₂"-wide first border strips to that measurement. Sew to top and bottom of quilt. Press seam toward first border.

5. Measure quilt through center from top to bottom including borders just added. Cut two 1¹/₂"-wide first border strips to that measurement. Sew to sides. Press.

6. Repeat steps 4 and 5 to join, fit, trim, and sew 1"-wide second border strips, 2"-wide third border strips, and 5¹/₂"-wide outside border strips to top, bottom, and sides. Press toward each newly added border.

7. Carefully remove paper patterns from flower blocks.

## Layering and Finishing

1. Cut backing crosswise into three equal pieces. Sew pieces together to make one 95" x 120" (approximate) backing piece. Cut backing to 95" x 105". Arrange and baste backing, batting, and top together referring to Layering the Quilt directions on page 80. (Run backing seams parallel to top and bottom edges of quilt top.)

2. Hand or machine quilt as desired.

3. Sew 2³/₄" x 42" binding strips together to make four pairs. Divide remaining two 2³/₄" x 42" binding strips in half, and sew one half to each pieced 2³/₄"-wide binding strip. Refer to Binding the Quilt directions on page 80 and bind quilt to finish.

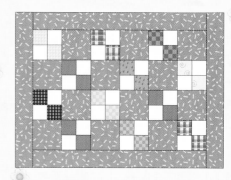

## DOUBLE FOUR-PATCH PILLOW SHAMS

*36" x 26"*
*Accent your bed quilt with this colorful pillow sham. Instructions are for one sham.*

Fabric A (Four-patch) - scraps to equal twenty-four 3" squares

Fabric B (Background) - ¹/₄ yard, cut into twenty-four 3" squares

Fabric C (Blocks) - ¹/₃ yard, cut into twelve 5¹/₂" squares

Outside Border - ¹/₂ yard, cut into four 3¹/₂" x 42" strips

Lining & Batting - 40" x 30"

Backing - 1¹/₂ yards, cut into two 26¹/₂" x 21" pieces

1. Make six Double Four-Patch Blocks following instructions on page 7 for steps 1-4.

2. Arrange blocks in two horizontal rows of three blocks each. Sew blocks into rows. Press seams in opposite directions from row to row.

3. Sew rows together.

4. Cut two 3¹/₂" x 30¹/₂" outside border strips and sew to top and bottom of unit from step 3.

5. Cut 3¹/₂" x 26¹/₂" outside border strips and sew to sides of unit from step 4.

6. Arrange and baste backing, batting, and top together. Quilt as desired. Trim batting and lining even with raw edge of pillow top.

7. Refer to Finishing the Pillow Cover instructions on page 70 to make the backing, replacing the 23¹/₂" x 14¹/₂" pieces with 26¹/₂" x 21" backing pieces. Overlap the backing panels to make a 36¹/₂" x 26¹/₂" piece.

8. Stitch in the ditch on the border seam to create a flange.

> "Where flowers bloom, so does hope."
>
> ~ Lady Bird Johnson

# Winsome Watering Cans

## Lap Quilt

### Splash your porch with color!

Splash your porch or sunroom with the vibrant colors and interesting details of the Winsome Watering Cans Lap Quilt. Hang this quilt on a wall above a much-loved vintage bench. Place a large terra cotta pot on one end of the bench and train an ivy or clematis to grow up a small trellis placed in the pot. This will add some softness and height to your grouping and visually link the two elements. Add painted watering cans, terra cotta pots filled with flowers, and some old garden implements to your bench for a garden-fresh approach to decorating.

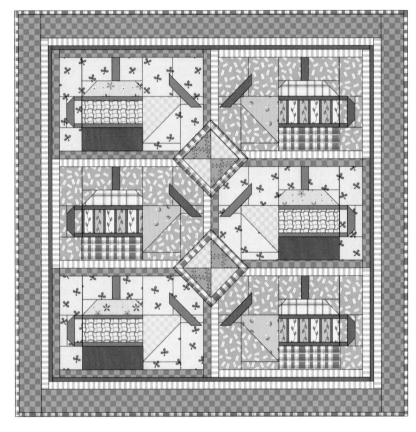

Winsome Watering Cans Lap Quilt

*Finished Size: 52" square*

*Photos: pages 15 and 18*

*April showers or not, the savvy gardener always keeps a watering can close by … just in case! Our delightful lap quilt features these trusty garden standbys in two different colorways, with some facing right and some facing left. Not to worry, if you follow the simple step-by-step instructions and try our efficient quick-piecing methods, you'll breeze right through.*

# Fabric Requirements and Cutting Instructions

Read all instructions before beginning and use ¹/₄"-wide seam allowances throughout. Read Cutting the Strips and Pieces on page 78 prior to cutting fabrics.

| | First Cut | | Second Cut | |
|---|---|---|---|---|
| | Number of Strips or Pieces | Dimensions | Number of Pieces | Dimensions |
| Fabric A Background<br>³/₄ yard of each of two different fabrics | 2 | 5¹/₂" x 42"<br>*Cut for each fabric* | 3<br>6 | 5¹/₂" squares<br>5¹/₂" x 4¹/₂" |
| | 2 | 3¹/₂" x 42"<br>*Cut for each fabric* | 3<br>3<br>3<br>6<br>3 | 3¹/₂" x 6¹/₂"<br>3¹/₂" x 5¹/₂"<br>3¹/₂" x 4¹/₂"<br>3¹/₂" squares<br>2¹/₂" squares |
| | 2 | 1¹/₂" x 42"<br>*Cut for each fabric* | 3<br>3<br>6<br>9 | 1¹/₂" x 5¹/₂"<br>1¹/₂" x 4¹/₂"<br>1¹/₂" x 3¹/₂"<br>1¹/₂" squares |
| Fabric B Can Top<br>¹/₈ yard each of two fabrics | 1 | 2¹/₂" x 42"<br>*Cut for each fabric* | 3 | 2¹/₂" x 8¹/₂" |
| Fabric C Handles, Can Accents, & Spout Tip<br>¹/₆ yard each of two fabrics | 2 | 1¹/₂" x 42"<br>*Cut for each fabric* | 3<br>3<br>3 | 1¹/₂" x 6¹/₂"<br>1¹/₂" x 4¹/₂"<br>1¹/₂" x 3¹/₂" |
| | 2 | 1" x 42"<br>*Cut for each fabric* | 6<br>6 | 1" x 8¹/₂"<br>1" x 1¹/₂" |
| Fabric D Can Center<br>¹/₈ yard each of two fabrics | 1 | 3¹/₂" x 42"<br>*Cut for each fabric* | 3 | 3¹/₂" x 8¹/₂" |
| Fabric E Can Bottom<br>¹/₈ yard each of two fabrics | 1 | 3¹/₂" x 42"<br>*Cut for each fabric* | 3 | 3¹/₂" x 8¹/₂" |
| Fabric F Spout<br>¹/₄ yard each of two fabrics | 1 | 5¹/₂" x 42"<br>*Cut for each fabric* | 3<br>6 | 5¹/₂" x 6¹/₂"<br>1¹/₂" squares |
| Fabric G Block Border<br>¹/₃ yard each of two fabrics | 6 | 1¹/₂" x 42"<br>*Cut for each fabric* | 6<br>6 | 1¹/₂" x 19¹/₂"<br>1¹/₂" x 14¹/₂" |
| Fabric H Center Square<br>¹/₈ yard each of two fabrics | 4 | 4¹/₄" squares<br>*Cut for each fabric* | | |
| Fabric I Center Square Border<br>¹/₃ yard | 8 | 5¹/₂" squares | | |

## Borders

| | | First Cut | |
|---|---|---|---|
| | | Number of Strips or Pieces | Dimensions |
| | Inside Border<br>¹/₆ yard | 5 | 1" x 42" |
| | Middle Border<br>¹/₄ yard | 5 | 1¹/₂" x 42" |
| | Outside Border<br>⁷/₈ yard | 5 | 3¹/₂" x 42" |
| | Binding<br>¹/₂ yard | 6 | 2³/₄" x 42" |

Backing - 3¹/₄ yards
Batting - 58" square

## Making the Blocks

You'll be making a total of six Watering Can Blocks: three each in two different colorways. You'll need one left-facing and two right-facing watering cans in the colorway for Block 1. You'll need two left-facing and one right-facing watering cans in the colorway for Block 2. Each block measures 19¹/₂" x 12¹/₂" before block borders are added.

Note: All diagrams show Block 1 colorway.

1. Refer to Quick Corner Triangle directions on page 78. Sew one 1½" Fabric A square and one 2½" Fabric A square to opposite corners of a 2½" x 8½" Fabric B piece as shown. Press seams toward triangles. Make one for Block 1 and two for Block 2.

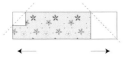

A = 1½ x 1½
A = 2½ x 2½
B = 2½ x 8½
Make 1 for Block 1
Make 2 for Block 2

2. Repeat step 1 to sew one 1½" Fabric A square and one 2½" Fabric A square to opposite corners of each remaining 2½" x 8½" Fabric B piece as shown. Press. Make two for Block 1 and one for Block 2.

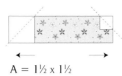

A = 1½ x 1½
A = 2½ x 2½
B = 2½ x 8½

Make 2 for Block 1
Make 1 for Block 2

3. Sew one 1½" x 3½" Fabric C piece between one 3½" Fabric A square and one 3½" x 4½" Fabric A piece as shown. Press. Make three each for Blocks 1 and 2.

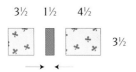

Make 3 for Block 1
Make 3 for Block 2

4. Sew one unit from step 3 to each unit from steps 1 and 2 as shown. Press. Make one left-facing and two right-facing units for Block 1. Make two left-facing and one right-facing units for Block 2.

  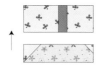

Make 1 for Block 1     Make 2 for Block 1
Make 2 for Block 2     Make 1 for Block 2

5. Sew one 1" x 8½" Fabric C piece, one 3½" x 8½" Fabric D piece, one 1" x 8½" Fabric C piece, and one 3½" x 8½" Fabric E piece as shown. Press. Make three each for Blocks 1 and 2.

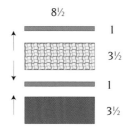

Make 3 for Block 1
Make 3 for Block 2

6. Sew one unit from step 4 to each unit from step 5 as shown. Press. Make one left-facing and two right-facing units for Block 1. Make two left-facing and one right-facing units for Block 2.

Make 1 for Block 1     Make 2 for Block 1
Make 2 for Block 2     Make 1 for Block 2

7. Sew one 1½" x 3½" Fabric A piece between two 1" x 1½" Fabric C pieces. Press. Make three each for Blocks 1 and 2.

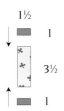

Make 3 for Block 1
Make 3 for Block 2

8. Refer to Quick Corner Triangle directions on page 78. Sew one 1½" Fabric A square to two corners of each 1½" x 4½" Fabric C piece as shown. Press. Make three each for Blocks 1 and 2.

A = 1½ x 1½
C = 1½ x 4½
Make 3 for Block 1
Make 3 for Block 2

**9.** Sew each unit from step 8 between one unit from step 7 and one 1½" x 4½" Fabric A piece. Press. Make three each for Blocks 1 and 2.

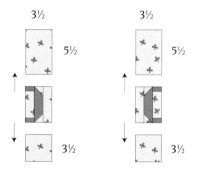

Make 3 for Block 1
Make 3 for Block 2

**10.** Sew one unit from step 9 between one 3½" x 5½" Fabric A piece and one 3½" Fabric A square as shown. Press. Make one left-facing and two right-facing units for Block 1. Make two left-facing and one right-facing units for Block 2.

Make 1 for Block 1   Make 2 for Block 1
Make 2 for Block 2   Make 1 for Block 2

**11.** Sew one unit from step 10 to each unit from step 6 as shown. Press. Make one left-facing and two right-facing units for Block 1. Make two left-facing and one right-facing units for Block 2.

Make 1 for Block 1   Make 2 for Block 1
Make 2 for Block 2   Make 1 for Block 2

12. Refer to Quick Corner Triangle directions on page 78. Sew one 5½" Fabric A square to one 5½" x 6½" Fabric F piece, aligning the bottom and side edges as shown. Press. Make one left-facing and two right-facing units for Block 1. Make two left-facing and one right-facing units for Block 2.

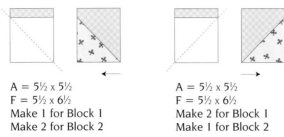

A = 5½ x 5½
F = 5½ x 6½
Make 1 for Block 1
Make 2 for Block 2

A = 5½ x 5½
F = 5½ x 6½
Make 2 for Block 1
Make 1 for Block 2

13. Sew each unit from step 12 to one 1½" x 5½" Fabric A piece as shown. Press. Make one left-facing and two right-facing units for Block 1. Make two left-facing and one right-facing units for Block 2.

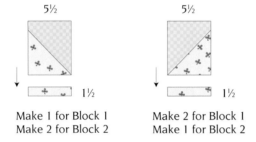

5½

5½

1½

1½

Make 1 for Block 1
Make 2 for Block 2

Make 2 for Block 1
Make 1 for Block 2

14. Refer to Quick Corner Triangle directions on page 78. Sew one 1½" Fabric F square to one corner of one 1½" x 3½" Fabric A piece as shown. Press. Make one left-facing and two right-facing units for block 1. Make two left-facing and one right-facing units for block 2.

F = 1½ x 1½
A = 1½ x 3½
Make 1 for Block 1
Make 2 for Block 2

F = 1½ x 1½
A = 1½ x 3½
Make 2 for Block 1
Make 1 for Block 2

15. Sew each unit from step 14 to one 3½" x 6½" Fabric A piece as shown. Press. Make one left-facing and two right-facing units for Block 1. Make two left-facing and one right-facing units for Block 2.

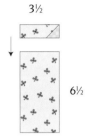

3½

6½

Make 1 for Block 1
Make 2 for Block 2

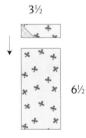

3½

6½

Make 2 for Block 1
Make 1 for Block 2

16. Sew each unit from step 15 to one unit from step 13 as shown. Press. Make one left-facing and two right-facing units for Block 1. Make two left-facing and one right-facing units for Block 2.

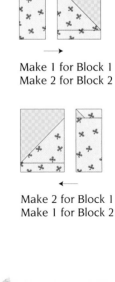

Make 1 for Block 1
Make 2 for Block 2

Make 2 for Block 1
Make 1 for Block 2

17. Refer to Quick Corner Triangle directions on page 78. Sew one 1½" Fabric F square to one corner of one 5½" x 4½" Fabric A piece as shown. Press seams away from triangle. Make one left-facing and two right-facing units for Block 1. Make two left-facing and one right-facing units for Block 2.

F = 1½ x 1½
A = 5½ x 4½
Make 1 for Block 1
Make 2 for Block 2

F = 1½ x 1½
A = 5½ x 4½
Make 2 for Block 1
Make 1 for Block 2

18. Sew each unit from step 17 to one 5½" x 4½" Fabric A piece as shown. Press. Make one left-facing and two right-facing units for Block 1. Make two left-facing and one right-facing units for Block 2.

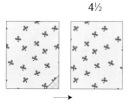

4½

5½

Make 1 for Block 1
Make 2 for Block 2

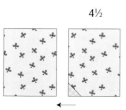

4½

Make 2 for Block 1
Make 1 for Block 2

19. Sew each unit from step 18 to one unit from step 16 as shown. Press. Make one left-facing and two right-facing units for Block 1. Make two left-facing and one right-facing units for Block 2.

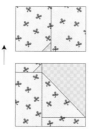

Make 1 for Block 1
Make 2 for Block 2
Make 2 reversed for Block 1 and 1 reversed for Block 2

20. Sew each unit from step 19 to one unit from step 11 as shown. Press. Make one left-facing as shown below and two right-facing units for Block 1. Make two left-facing (as shown) and one right-facing units for Block 2.

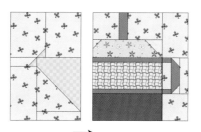

21. Press ¼" under along the long edges of each 1½" x 6½" Fabric C strip. Press corners under at a 45 degree angle as shown and trim, leaving ¼" seam allowance. Refer to Hand Appliqué directions on page 79 and quilt layout on page 12. Use preferred method to appliqué appropriately colored spout tip on each block.

## Block Borders

1. Sew matching 1½" x 19½" Fabric G block borders to top and bottom of each Block 1. Press seams toward borders. Repeat to sew matching 1½" x 19½" Fabric G block borders to top and bottom of each Block 2. Press.

2. Sew matching 1½" x 14½" Fabric G block borders to sides of each Block 1. Press seams toward borders. Repeat to sew matching 1½" x 14½" Fabric G block borders to sides of each Block 2. Press.

3. Refer to Quick Corner Triangle directions on page 78. Sew one 4¼" Fabric H square to one corner of each 5½" Fabric I square as shown to make two sets of four matching center squares. In one set, press seams toward Fabric H. In other set, press seams toward Fabric I.

H = 4¼ x 4¼
I = 5½ x 5½
Make 4 each color

4. Refer to Quick Corner Triangle directions on page 78 and quilt layout on page 12. Sew matching center squares from step 3 to lower right corner of one right-facing Block 1, upper right corner of other right-facing Block 1, and both upper and lower left corners of left-facing Block 1. Be sure center square is oriented with Fabric I triangle at corner of block as shown in step 5. Press.

5. Repeat to sew matching center squares to lower left corner of left-facing Block 2, upper left corner of other left-facing Block 2, and upper and lower right corners of right-facing Block 2. Press.

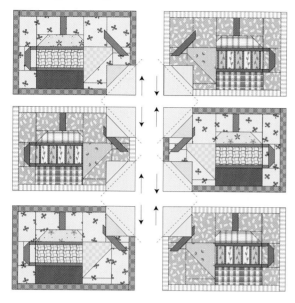

## Assembly

1. Refer to quilt layout on page 12 and color photos on pages 15 and 18. Arrange three horizontal rows of two blocks each. Note that each row contains one each of Block 1 and Block 2. Sew blocks together into rows. Press in opposite directions from row to row.

2. Sew rows together. Press.

3. Sew 1" x 42" inside border strips end to end to make one continuous 1"-wide strip. Measure quilt through center from side to side. Trim two 1"-wide inside border strips to that measurement. Sew to top and bottom. Press toward border strip.

4. Measure quilt through center from top to bottom, including borders just added. Trim two 1"-wide inside border strips to that measurement. Sew to sides. Press.

5. Repeat steps 3 and 4 to join, fit, trim, and sew 1½"-wide middle border strips to top, bottom, and sides of quilt. Press toward middle border.

6. Repeat steps 3 and 4 to join, fit, trim, and sew 3½"-wide outside border strips to top, bottom, and sides of quilt. Press toward outside border.

## Layering and Finishing

1. Cut backing crosswise into two equal pieces. Sew pieces together to make one 58½" x 84" (approximate) backing piece. Cut backing to 58½" x 58½". Arrange and baste backing, batting, and top together referring to Layering the Quilt directions on page 80.

2. Hand or machine quilt as desired.

3. Cut two 2¾" x 42" binding strips in half crosswise and sew one piece to each remaining 2¾" x 42" binding strip. Refer to Binding the Quilt directions on page 80 and bind quilt to finish.

# WATERING CAN PLACEMATS

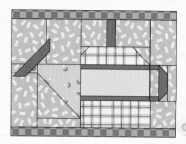

*19" x 14"*
*Decorate your table with watering cans! These watering can blocks are the perfect size for placemats. To make six placemats, follow these simple instructions.*

For Fabric Requirements and Cutting Instructions, follow the chart on page 13 for Fabrics A through F. For Block Border, Fabric G, reduce amount to ⅙ yard for each fabric and cut only the 1½" x 19½" pieces. Add 1½ yards of backing fabric cut into six 15" x 20" pieces.

1. Construct six watering can blocks following steps 1-21, referring to pages 14-17.

2. Sew 1½" x 19½" border pieces to the top and bottom of block. Press. Block size will be 19½" x 14½".

3. Cut six pieces of backing fabric and six pieces of batting to 15" x 20".

4. Position top and backing right sides together. Center both pieces on top of batting and pin all three layers together. Using ¼"-wide seams, sew around edges, leaving a 5" opening for turning.

5. Trim backing and batting to same size as top. Trim corners and turn right side out. Hand stitch opening closed. Press.

6. Hand or machine quilt as desired.

# FRUIT & FLOWERS

## Wall Quilt

Fruit & Flowers Wall Quilt
*Finished size 24" x 14½"*
*Photo page 21*

> "All the flowers
> of all the
> tomorrows are
> in the seeds
> of today."
>
> ~ Indian Proverb

### Big Decorating punch in a small package!

The small size of the Fruit and Flowers Wall Quilt makes this quilt the perfect accent for any room in your home. Hang it in the kitchen and group it with a basket of fresh fruit. Mount it on a piece of black foam core and place it on a small easel or large plate rack for a dramatic accent to your buffet or sideboard. It would be lovely grouped with delicately painted china. Attach it to a vintage window and hang it on a wall of your porch or sunroom for even more dimension. This quilt would also make a sweet accent pillow for a chair or bed.

*Nature's rich bounty provides a fitting focal point for this luscious—and colorful—wallhanging. Our instructions call for quick-as-a-wink fused appliqué, but you can substitute more traditional hand appliqué methods if you wish. See page 23 for information on where to find the just-right strawberry buttons.*

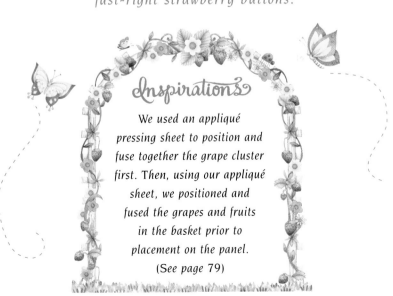

### Inspirations

*We used an appliqué pressing sheet to position and fuse together the grape cluster first. Then, using our appliqué sheet, we positioned and fused the grapes and fruits in the basket prior to placement on the panel.*

(See page 79)

## Fabric Requirements and Cutting Instructions

Read all instructions before beginning and use 1/4"-wide seam allowances throughout. Read Cutting the Strips and Pieces on page 78 prior to cutting fabrics.

| | | First Cut | | Second Cut | |
| --- | --- | --- | --- | --- | --- |
| | | Number of Strips or Pieces | Dimensions | Number of Pieces | Dimensions |
| | Fabric A Background 1/3 yard | 1 | 9" x 19 1/2" | | |
| | Fabric B Grass 1/8 yard | 1 | 1 1/2" x 42" | 1 | 1 1/2" x 19 1/2" |
| Borders | | | | | |
| | Accent Border 1/8 yard | 3 | 1" x 42" | | |
| | Outside Border 1/4 yard | 3 | 2 1/2" x 42" | | |
| Appliqués (basket, fruits, flowers & leaves) - scraps<br>Backing - 1/2 yard<br>Batting - 28" x 18" | | | Heavyweight Fusible Web - 1/4 yard<br>Strawberry Buttons - 9<br>Embroidery Floss - green | | |

## Assembling the Center Panel

The instructions given are for the quick-fuse appliqué method. If you prefer traditional hand appliqué, be sure to reverse all appliqué templates and add 1/4" seam allowances when cutting appliqué pieces. Refer to Hand Appliqué directions on page 79 for additional guidance as needed.

1. Sew 9" x 19 1/2" Fabric A background piece and 1 1/2" x 19 1/2" Fabric B grass strip together. Press toward Fabric B.

2. Refer to Quick-Fuse Appliqué directions on page 78. Trace appliqué patterns on pages 22-23 for basket, fruits, flowers, stems, and leaves.

3. Trace words on page 23 on tissue and roughly cut around the words. Refer to layout and position appliqués and words on panel. When satisfied with placement, fuse appliqués in place.

4. Transfer words to appliquéd panel. Using three strands of embroidery floss, stitch words with a running or stem stitch. Refer to Embroidery Stitch Guide on page 78.

5. Using three strands of embroidery floss, stitch tendrils and other fruit details with a running or stem stitch as desired. Refer to Embroidery Stitch Guide on page 78.

## Borders

1. Sew one 1" x 42" accent border strip and one 2 1/2" x 42" outside border strip together to make a border unit. Press toward outside border strip. Make three border units.

2. Refer to Mitered Borders directions on page 80 and use border units from step 1 to fit, trim, and sew border units to top, bottom, and sides. Miter corners. Press.

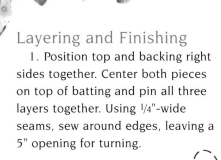

## Layering and Finishing

**1.** Position top and backing right sides together. Center both pieces on top of batting and pin all three layers together. Using 1/4"-wide seams, sew around edges, leaving a 5" opening for turning.

**2.** Trim backing and batting to same size as top. Trim corners, turn right side out, hand stitch opening closed, and press.

**3.** Hand or machine quilt as desired.

**4.** Referring to quilt layout, page 20, and photo page 21, sew nine strawberry buttons to quilt as shown.

Strawberry Buttons
Mill Hill/Gay Bowles Sales, Inc.
(800) 356-9438, www.millhill.com
43179 Set of Three (one each size)
43176 Set of Two (large strawberry)
43177 Set of Two (medium strawberry)
43178 Set of Two (small strawberry)

From the Flower

Comes the Fruit

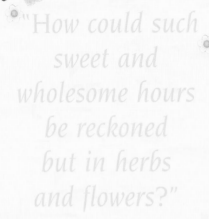

# BERRIES & VINES
## Window Boxes

### Think outside the box!

Mix textures and techniques by adding a few painted pieces to accent your favorite textiles. We used tin flower boxes for our painted projects, but you could also paint terra cotta pots or planters, or wooden shelves or furniture. The same basic techniques will work, just be sure to prepare your surface appropriately for the project you select.

Of course, plants would be beautiful in your window boxes, but why not think outside the box! Use window boxes to hold folded floral fabrics in your sewing room, recipe books in your kitchen, toiletries or towels in the bathroom, or magazines in the guest room!

Berries Window Box

Vines Window Box

What could be sweeter for your patio or porch than these whimsical window boxes? We used two different techniques and patterns for our window boxes to give you lots of ideas for painting your own projects to match your floral creations. The strawberry window box features dimensional berries and leaves on a checkerboard background. The yellow window box features a simple leaf and vine pattern that is easy even for a novice painter.

## Materials Needed For Both Boxes

Tin or wood window boxes
Sandpaper
Flat spray primer or
  all-purpose sealer
Acrylic craft paints in a variety of
  colors (dark green, medium green,
  light green, red, black, antique
  gold, and medium yellow)
Sea sponge
Assorted paintbrushes
1" checkerboard stencil and brush
One thin sheet of craft tin
Fine gauge green florist wire
Heavy gauge wire
Epoxy glue
Graphite paper
Crackle Medium
Spray matte varnish
Tracing paper

## Painting the Window Boxes

### Preparing the surface

Prepare tin window boxes by sanding lightly, if needed, then spray with flat primer. Allow primer to dry thoroughly. Prepare wood window box by sanding lightly then coating box with an all-purpose sealer.

### Berries Window Box

*Refer to the color photo as needed.*

1. Base coat all sides of window box with medium green acrylic paint. Allow to dry thoroughly.

2. Using sea sponge, sponge light green acrylic paint over basecoat. Blot your sponge on paper before applying paint to window box and work sponge lightly with a tapping motion until light green sponging is well blended over basecoat. Dry thoroughly.

3. Using a 1" checkerboard stencil and stencil brush, stencil medium green checks on front side of window box. Be sure to place your stencil in such a way that checks are centered in the available space. Allow to dry thoroughly.

4. Refer to strawberry vine pattern on page 23 for layout suggestion. Enlarge strawberry and leaf pattern to the size appropriate for your window box, then transfer leaf and strawberry patterns to a sheet of craft tin. Carefully cut out berries and leaves using heavy duty scissors. Bend slightly to give berries and leaves some dimension.

5. Spray with metal primer and allow to dry. Using acrylic paints, paint berries red and leaves and berry caps green. It may require two coats of paint to completely cover primer. When this base coat is dry, add small black dashes to strawberries to simulate seeds and add veins to leaves.

6. Cut four pieces of light gauge wire into 6" pieces and wrap around a pencil to curl.

7. Cut pieces of heavy gauge wire for stems and bend into shape following appliqué pattern on page 23.

8. Refer to photo and glue all elements into place using epoxy glue.

9. Spray completed window box with several coats of spray matte varnish, following manufacturer's directions. Use marine varnish if you intend to use the planter outdoors.

### Vines Window Box

1. Base coat all sides of window box with light antique gold paint. Dry thoroughly.

2. Following manufacturer's directions, apply crackle medium over basecoat. Allow to "set" according to manufacturer's specifications. Apply a very thin coat where leaves are to be painted.

3. Apply a quick, even coat of medium yellow paint over window box. Crackle will appear in freshly painted surface. Do not touch, as surface is very fragile when wet. Dry thoroughly.

4. Using green paint and referring to photo, paint a wavy line across top part of box.

5. Enlarge or reduce leaf appliqué #15 pattern on page 48 to fit your window box. Using graphite paper, transfer leaf pattern to window box, placing leaves where desired along vine. A purchased leaf stencil will also work.

6. Paint leaves green. Add a slightly darker green vein to each leaf.

7. Paint an accent color around top edge of window box.

8. Spray completed window box with several coats of s... varnish, following ma... directions. Use marine... intend to use planter ou...

Berry and Leaf templates for Berries Window Box

# FRIENDSHIP

"More things *grow in the garden* than the *gardener* sows."

— *Spanish Proverb*

Playful pansies nod their
sweet-faced heads
And friends gather to share
joyful conversation and tea.
An English garden is spread
with toast and jam
And the garden's bounty is plain to see.

PANSIES & TEA

# PANSIES & TEA

*Wall Quilt*

**Pansies & Tea Wall Quilt**
*Finished size: 23" x 21"*
*Photo Page 29*

*Dainty, dimensional pansies dress this delightful wall quilt,
perfect for any setting where a bit of whimsy is "on the menu."
Tiny buttons and simple embroidery stitches
add effortless, but effective, detail.*

*"Friends are
the flowers in
life's garden."*

~ *From an early 1900's Sampler*

### A Natural with Teapots!

Have a teapot collection? This wall quilt is a natural to group with your teapots. Hang it low over a table or buffet and group teapots and cups and saucers around it. Use vintage tea boxes to raise a few of your teapots and make sure your cups and saucers are a variety of sizes and patterns. Place one cup and saucer on a side table and fill it with pansies. Or, try displaying your teapot collection on an old metal plant stand and hang your wall quilt nearby.

## Fabric Requirements and Cutting Instructions

Read all instructions before beginning and use 1/4"-wide seam allowances throughout. Read Cutting the Strips and Pieces on page 78 prior to cutting fabrics.

| | First Cut | | Second Cut | |
| --- | --- | --- | --- | --- |
| | Number of Strips or Pieces | Dimensions | Number of Pieces | Dimensions |
| Background 1/2 yard | 1 | 14 1/2" x 12 1/2" | | |
| Teapots, Cups and Saucers *scraps* | | | | |
| Pansies and Leaves *scraps* | | | | |
| Inside Border 1/8 yard | 2 | 1 1/2" x 42" | 4 | 1 1/2" x 14 1/2" |
| Middle Border 1/8 yard | 2 | 1" x 42" | 2 | 1" x 16 1/2" |
| | | | 2 | 1" x 15 1/2" |
| Outside Border 1/4 yard | 2 | 3" x 42" | 2 | 3" x 20 1/2" |
| | | | 2 | 3" x 17 1/2" |
| Binding 1/3 yard | 3 | 2 3/4" x 42" | | |

Backing - 3/4 yard (One 27" x 25" piece)
Batting - 27" x 25"
Three Assorted Buttons - 1/4"–3/8"
Perle Cotton or Embroidery Floss
Lightweight Fusible Web - 1/3 yard
Heavyweight Fusible Web - 2/3 yard
Ceramic Pansy Button - optional (see page 31)

## Appliquéing Center Panel

The instructions given are for the quick-fuse appliqué method. If you prefer traditional hand appliqué, be sure to reverse teapot appliqué templates, and add 1/4"-wide seam allowances when cutting appliqué pieces. Refer to Hand Appliqué directions on page 79 for additional guidance as needed.

1. Refer to Quick-Fuse Appliqué directions on page 78. Trace appliqué patterns on pages 30-31 for teapot (A-O) and teacup (P-U) appliqués. Use assorted scraps to trace and cut one each of pieces A-O, and two each (one regular and one reverse) of pieces P-U. Use lightweight fusible web.

2. Refer to quilt layout on page 28 and position appliqués on background piece. Fuse appliqués in place and finish edges as desired.

## Assembly

1. Sew 1 1/2" x 14 1/2" inside border strips to top and bottom of 12 1/2" x 14 1/2" background piece. Press seams toward inside border. Repeat to sew remaining 1 1/2" x 14 1/2" inside border strips to sides. Press.

2. Repeat step 1 to sew 1" x 16 1/2" middle border strips to top and bottom, and 1" x 15 1/2" middle border strips to sides. Press seams toward middle border.

3. Repeat step 1 to sew 3" x 17 1/2" outside border strips to top and bottom, and 3" x 20 1/2" outside border strips to sides. Press seams toward outside border.

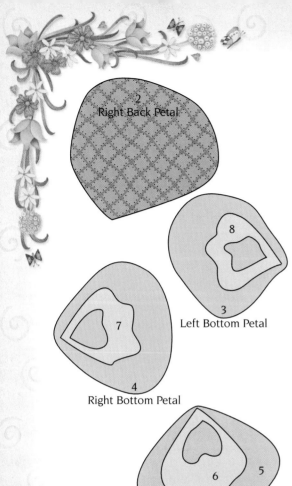

Right Back Petal 2

8
Left Bottom Petal 3

7
4
Right Bottom Petal

6 5
Center Bottom Petal

1
Left Back Petal

9
Leaf

1
Left Back

2
Right Back

4
Right Bottom

3
Left Bottom

5
Center Bottom

Placement diagram-
tack in numerical order

## Layering and Finishing

**1.** Arrange and baste backing, batting, and top together referring to Layering the Quilt directions on page 80.

**2.** Hand or machine quilt as desired.

**3.** Draw steam on appliquéd panel, referring to quilt layout on page 28. Use perle cotton or three strands of embroidery floss to stitch steam with a running stitch over each teacup. Refer to Embroidery Stitch Guide on page 78.

**4.** Press a piece of heavyweight fusible web to wrong side of each piece of fabric to be used for pansy petals and leaves. We used an 8" x 5" scrap for each pair of petals (left and right back petal and left and right bottom petal), 4" square for bottom center petal, and 6" x 5" scrap for three leaves. Remove paper backing from fusible web, fold each fabric scrap in half crosswise, fusible sides together. Press.

**5.** Use patterns on this page to trace and cut one of each back petal (left and right) on each folded and fused back petal scrap, one of each bottom petal (left and right) from each folded and fused bottom petal scrap, one bottom center petal from each folded and fused bottom center scrap, and two or three leaves from each folded and fused leaf fabric.

**6.** Refer to Quick-Fuse Appliqué directions on page 78. Trace appliqué patterns on this page for pansy centers 6, 7, and 8. Cut three of each piece, using assorted scraps and heavyweight fusible web. Refer to placement diagram on this page and position appliqués on appropriate bottom petals. Fuse appliqués in place.

**7.** Refer to quilt layout on page 28, and tack each pansy petal and leaf to quilt with matching colored thread. Stitch a 1/4"–3/8" small button in center of each pansy. If desired, sew a pansy button to the teapot lid (see page 31.)

**8.** Sew 2³/4" x 42" binding strips end to end to make one continuous 2³/4"-wide binding strip. Refer to Binding the Quilt directions on page 80 and bind quilt to finish.

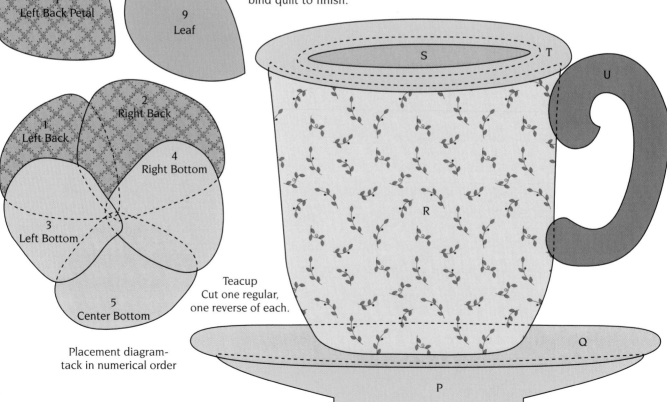

Teacup
Cut one regular,
one reverse of each.

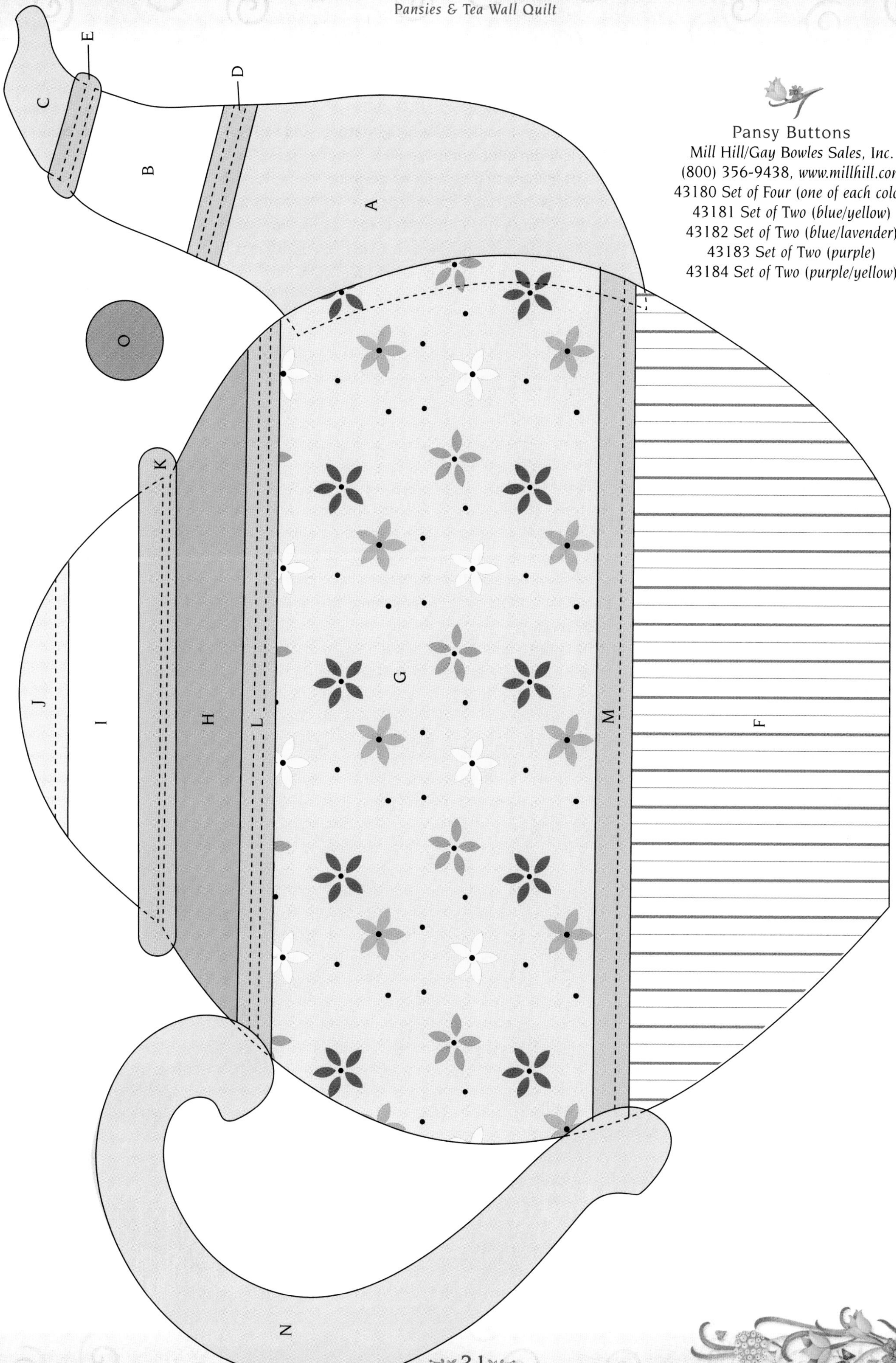

C

E

D

B

A

**Pansy Buttons**
Mill Hill/Gay Bowles Sales, Inc.
(800) 356-9438, *www.millhill.com*
43180 *Set of Four (one of each color)*
43181 *Set of Two (blue/yellow)*
43182 *Set of Two (blue/lavender)*
43183 *Set of Two (purple)*
43184 *Set of Two (purple/yellow)*

O

K

J

I

H

L

G

M

F

N

### Perky Pansies Add Decorating Punch

The pretty faces of these pansies will brighten any room! Use this valance in the kitchen and place several flowerpots filled with pansies on the windowsill. Make one or two single pansies to use as potholders and hang them on pegs for all to see. Decorate the guest bathroom with a pansy theme and use this valance as a topper for your shower curtain or bathroom window. Pick up the bright colors of the pansies in your towels.

# PIECED PANSY
## Window Valance

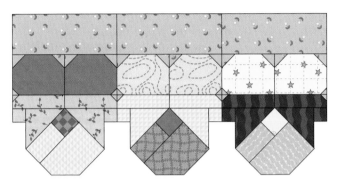

**Pieced Pansy Window Valance**
*Finished Size for each pansy panel: 8" x 12"*
*Photo: page 34*

Here's a clever twist on the traditional pansy-filled window box: top your window with a valance of fabric pansies instead! Yardage and instructions are for a single pansy panel, but you can custom fit the valance to your décor by making as many panels as you wish.

## Fabric Requirements and Cutting Instructions

Read all instructions before beginning and use 1/4"-wide seam allowances throughout. Read Cutting the Strips and Pieces on page 78 prior to cutting fabrics.

| Fabric required for each pansy | First Cut | |
|---|---|---|
| | Number of Strips or Pieces | Dimensions |
| Fabric A Background 1/8 yard | 1 | 3 1/2" x 8 1/2" |
| | 4 | 1 1/2" squares |
| | 4 | 1" squares |
| Fabric B Top Petals scraps | 2 | 3 1/2" x 4 1/2" |
| Fabric C Middle Petals scraps | 1 | 3 7/8" square |
| | 2 | 1 1/2" x 4 1/2" |
| | 2 | 1 1/2" squares |
| Fabric D Bottom Petals scraps | 1 | 3 1/4" x 4 3/4" |
| | 1 | 3 1/4" x 2" |
| Fabric E Pansy Center scraps | 1 | 2" square |

Backing - 10" x 14"
Batting - 10" x 14"
*Amounts are for one pansy only. Increase by number of pansies desired.*

## Making the Pansy Panel

**1.** Refer to Quick Corner Triangle directions on page 78. Sew two 1 1/2" Fabric A squares to both top corners of one 3 1/2" x 4 1/2" Fabric B piece as shown. Press. Sew one 1" Fabric A square to lower left corner of unit as shown. Press.

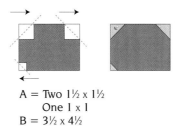

A = Two 1 1/2 x 1 1/2
One 1 x 1
B = 3 1/2 x 4 1/2

**2.** Repeat step 1 to sew two 1 1/2" Fabric A squares to both top corners of remaining 3 1/2" x 4 1/2" Fabric B piece. Sew one 1" Fabric A square to lower right corner of unit as shown. Press.

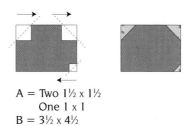

A = Two 1 1/2 x 1 1/2
One 1 x 1
B = 3 1/2 x 4 1/2

**3.** Refer to Quick Corner Triangle directions on page 78. Sew one 1" Fabric A square to upper left corner of one 1 1/2" x 4 1/2" Fabric C piece. Press.

A = 1 x 1
C = 1 1/2 x 4 1/2

## TEA PARTY GARDEN HAT

*Accent your flower-fresh tea party setting with this blossom bedecked garden hat. Wired French ribbon is the secret to these pretty flowers.*

**Ribbon Pansies**-1 yard each of assorted 1" and 1 1/2"-wide shaded wired French ribbon (12" lengths)
**Leaves**-1 yard each of assorted 1 1/2"-wide wired French ribbon
**Pansy buttons**-3 (see page 31)
**Purchased Hat**

**1.** Fold ribbon as shown. Hand baste along stitching line using about a 1/8"-long stitch. Vary the length and width of the ribbons to obtain different size pansies.

**2.** Pull stitches to gather, folding ribbon ends in toward center. Tack ends together around gathered center. Pansy is complete. For an added effect, sew a pansy button or add a smaller ribbon pansy to the flower center.

**3.** To make the leaf, cut 1 1/2"-wide ribbon to a 6"-length and fold in half crosswise. Hand baste along stitch line.

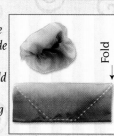

Fold

**4.** Pull stitches to gather and tack securely. Gently pull ends to sharpen points and bend wire to desired look. Trim excess ribbon.

**5.** Refer to color photo for pansy and leaf placement. Tack stitch the ribbon flowers and leaves in place.

**4.** Repeat step 3, sewing one 1" Fabric A square to upper right corner of remaining 1½" x 4½" Fabric C piece. Press.

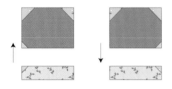

A = 1 x 1
C = 1½ x 4½

**5.** Sew unit from step 1 to unit from step 3 as shown. Press. Sew unit from step 2 to unit from step 4 as shown. Press.

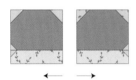

**6.** Sew units from step 5 together. Press seam open.

**7.** Sew 3¼" x 2" Fabric D piece to 2" Fabric E square. Press.

3¼    2

2

**8.** Sew 3¼" x 4¾" Fabric D piece to unit from step 7 as shown. Press. Measure 2" in both directions from lower left corner of unit and trim as shown.

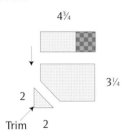

4¾

2

3¼

Trim   2

**9.** Cut 3⅞" Fabric C square in half once diagonally to make two triangles. Sew one triangle to each right angle edge of unit from step 8. Press toward triangles as shown.

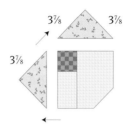

3⅞   3⅞

3⅞

**10.** Sew unit from step 9 between two 1½" Fabric C squares, aligning them along top edges as shown. Press.

1½    1½

1½

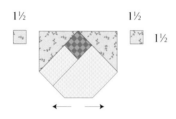

**11.** Sew unit from step 6 to unit from step 10. Press seam open.

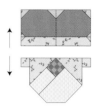

**12.** Sew 3½" x 8½" Fabric A piece to unit from step 11 as shown. Press. Note: As you make additional panels, press this seam in opposite directions from panel to panel.

8½

3½

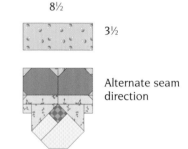

Alternate seam direction

**13.** Repeat steps 1-12 to make desired number of pansy panels.

## Layering and Finishing

**1.** Refer to valance layout on page 32 and color photo. Arrange and sew together desired number of pansy panels. Press seams open. Measure pansy valance and cut backing and batting to approximate width and length.

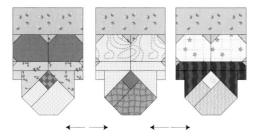

**2.** Position top and backing right sides together. Center both pieces on top of batting and pin all three layers together. Using ¼"-wide seams, sew around sides and lower edges, leaving top edge open for turning.

**3.** Trim backing to same size as top. Trim batting close to seam line to reduce bulk. Clip or notch corners, turn right side out. Press.

**4.** Hand or machine quilt as desired.

**5.** Referring to photo, use embroidery floss to stitch a large running stitch from lower point of pansy center to bottom of petal. Refer to Embroidery Stitch Guide on page 78. Gather loosely to create appearance of a curved bottom petal. Embroider French knots in pansy center.

**6.** To hang valance, cut fabric strip 3" to 4"-wide (depending on width of rod) by full length of valance, add 1". (You can use leftover background fabric or any coordinating piece.) Turn under ¼" hem on each short end. Turn under again, press, and stitch. Stitch curtain rod sleeve to top front of valance, right sides together, with ¼"-wide seam. Press seam toward sleeve. Turn raw edge of sleeve under ¼" and press. Turn sleeve to back of quilt and press.

**7.** Pin lower edge of sleeve to back of valance. Use matching thread to top stitch ¼" away from top edge of valance through panel and sleeve. Use invisible stitch to secure bottom edge of sleeve to valance. Insert rod through sleeve to hang.

## PRETTY PANSY TEA TRAY

*Your favorite teapot and teatime delicacies will look even more delectable when placed on this decorative tray. Hand-made rice paper provides a subtle backdrop for an arrangement of pressed flowers under glass.*

Unfinished wood tray
Wood sealer
Acrylic paint in medium blue
Paintbrushes
Spray matte varnish
Decorative hand-made rice paper*
Sheet of glass**
Variety of pressed flowers and foliage - (page 59)

*1.* Lightly sand wood tray and use a tack cloth to remove all sanding residue. Brush on wood sealer and allow to dry thoroughly.

*2.* Basecoat entire tray with medium blue acrylic paint. Several coats of paint may be required for a smooth finish. Dry thoroughly after each coat.

*3.* Spray tray with matte varnish to protect the paint. Dry thoroughly.

*4.* Cut decorative rice paper to the inside measurement of tray and set in place.

*5.* Arrange pressed flowers and leaves as desired on rice paper. Working one flower at a time and handling with tweezers, put a small drop of glue behind each element and set in place. Allow to dry. The glue will keep the flowers in place. Clean the glass. Handling carefully to avoid fingerprints, place the piece of glass on top of flowers and rice paper. The weight of the glass will serve to keep the rice paper and flowers in place. Enjoy your decorative tea tray! To clean, wipe glass with a damp cloth. Do not allow moisture to seep behind the glass.

*Available at art supply stores
**Have glass shop cut to fit inside tray and seam edges

# ENGLISH GARDEN
## Table Quilt

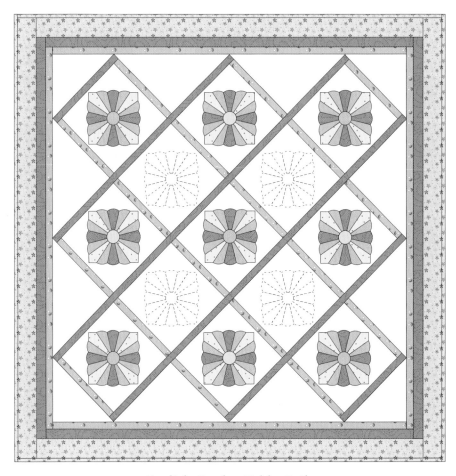

**English Garden Table Quilt**
*Finished size 69" square*
*Photo page 39*

*"What grows in the garden, so lovely and rare? Roses and dahlias and people grow there."*

~ A Gardener's Diary

### Perfect in Lots of Places

Although perfect on your summertime table, don't pigeonhole this quilt! It's a great size to use as a bed topper or lap quilt. Layer it with a solid-color bedspread or a compatible quilt on top of your bed for a fresh new look. Drape it on a white wicker settee for some Victorian ambiance. Use one of the Dresden Plate Blocks to make a pillow, or use three of the blocks for a table runner. This versatile pattern has stood the test of time and is sure to become an heirloom in your home.

*Afternoon refreshment assumes a festive air when you dress your table in this pretty pastel topper. Darling Dresden Plate posies bloom on crisp tone-on-tone backgrounds, while alternate blocks allow you to showcase your very best quilting stitches. You'll soon be ready to don your favorite flowered hat and invite your quilting friends to tea!*

## Fabric Requirements and Cutting Instructions

Read all instructions before beginning and use 1/4"-wide seam allowances throughout. Read Cutting the Strips and Pieces on page 78 prior to cutting fabrics.

| | First Cut | | Second Cut | |
|---|---|---|---|---|
| | Number of Strips or Pieces | Dimensions | Number of Pieces | Dimensions |
| Fabric A Background 2 1/2 yards | 1 | 19 3/4" x 42" | 2 | 19 3/4" squares |
| | 5 | 12 1/2" x 42" | 13 | 12 1/2" squares |
| | | | 2 | 10 7/8" squares |
| Fabric B Sashing 1/3 yard | 6 | 1 1/2" x 42" | 18 | 1 1/2" x 12 1/2" |
| Fabric C Sashing 3/8 yard | 7 | 1 1/2" x 42" | 2 | 1 1/2" x 40 1/2" |
| | | | 2 | 1 1/2" x 14 1/2" |
| Fabric D Wedge 1 1 yard | 72 | Use pattern to cut 36 and 36 reversed. | | |
| Fabric E Wedge 2 5/8 yard | 36 | Use pattern to cut. | | |
| Fabric F Plate Points 7/8 yard | 36 | Use pattern to cut. | | |
| Center Circles assorted scraps | 9 | 3" squares | | |
| **Borders** | | | | |
| Accent Border 3/8 yard | 7 | 1 1/2" x 42" | | |
| Middle Border 1/2 yard | 7 | 2" x 42" | | |
| Outside Border 3/4 yard | 7 | 3 1/2" x 42" | | |
| Binding 3/4 yard | 8 | 2 3/4" x 42" | | |

Backing - 4 1/3 yards
Batting - 76" x 76"
Template Plastic

## Assembly

**1.** Sew one 12 1/2" Fabric A square between two 1 1/2" x 12 1/2" Fabric B pieces as shown. Press. Make nine.

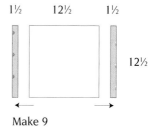

Make 9

**2.** Sew one 12 1/2" Fabric A square between two units from step 1 as shown. Press. Make two.

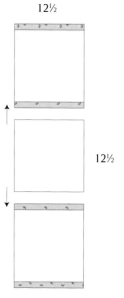

Make 2

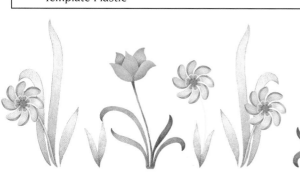

**3.** Sew one unit from step 1, one 12½" Fabric A square, one unit from step 1, one 12½"" Fabric A square, and one unit from step 1 in order shown. Press.

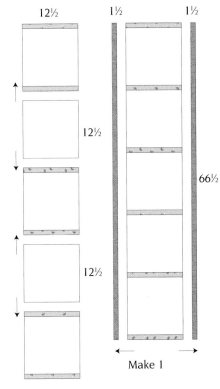

Make 1

**4.** Sew four 1½" x 42" Fabric C strips together end to end to make one continuous 1½"-wide strip. From this strip, cut two 1½" x 66½" sashing strips. Sew one sashing strip to each long side of unit from step 3 as shown in above diagram. Press.

**5.** Sew one 1½" x 40½" Fabric C sashing strip to one long side of each unit from step 2. Press. Make two.

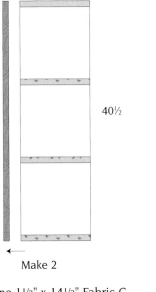

Make 2

**6.** Sew one 1½" x 14½" Fabric C sashing strip to each remaining unit from step 1 as shown. Press. Make two.

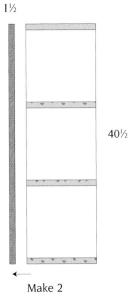

Make 2

**7.** Cut each 19¾" Fabric A background square in half twice diagonally to make four side setting triangles. Sew one unit from step 6 between two side setting triangles, taking care to position triangles as shown. Press. Make two.

Make 2

**8.** Sew one unit from step 5 between two remaining side setting triangles. Press. Make two.

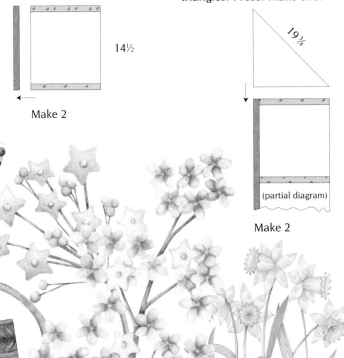

(partial diagram)

Make 2

**9.** Cut each 10⅞" Fabric A background square in half once diagonally to make two corner setting triangles. Sew one triangle to each unit from step 7, taking care to position triangle as shown. Press. Make two.

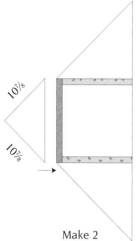

Make 2

**10.** Sew unit from step 4 between two remaining corner setting triangles. Press.

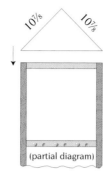

(partial diagram)

**11.** Quilt is assembled in diagonal rows. Refer to quilt layout on page 36 and color photo. Arrange units from steps 8, 9, and 10. Sew rows together. Press. Square quilt top as necessary, making sure to leave ¼" seam allowance on all edges.

# FRAMED FLOWERS

*Create a tiny botanical garden in a frame with this charming wall piece. Delicate pressed flowers and foliage are displayed in a whimsical arrangement. Used singly or as a grouping, these framed flowers will add summery charm all year long.*

Wooden picture frame
Wood sealer
Acrylic paint in medium green
Decorative paper in a subtle
   botanical print
Pressed flowers and
   leaves - (page 59)
White glue
Cardboard backing

*1. Lightly sand frame and apply sealer. Dry thoroughly.*

*2. Paint frame with a medium green acrylic paint. It may take several coats to achieve a smooth finish. Dry thoroughly.*

*3. Select a scrapbook paper, wrapping paper, or even wallpaper as your background. Look for an over-all subtle print. Scrapbook paper is the best choice as it is acid and lignin-free and your arrangement will last longer. Cut background paper to fit in your frame.*

*4. Arrange pressed flowers and leaves as desired on background paper. Using tweezers and placing one flower at a time, put a small drop of glue behind each flower to attach it to the background. Dry thoroughly.*

*5. Place flower arrangement carefully on glass in picture frame.*

*6. Cut cardboard to size and place behind the arrangement. Fasten in place using small nails or push points. Hang as desired.*

## Making Dresden Plates

You will be making nine Dresden Plates and appliquéing them to alternating Fabric A background blocks. The instructions given are for traditional hand appliqué. If you prefer the quick-fuse appliqué method, refer to Quick-Fuse Appliqué directions on page 78 for additional guidance as needed.

1. Trace patterns below onto template plastic and cut out. Before tracing templates on fabric, remember to space at least 1/2" apart on all sides. Trace seventy-two (thirty-six regular and thirty-six reverse) Wedge 1 from Fabric D, thirty-six Wedge 2 from Fabric E, thirty-six plate points from Fabric F, and nine center circles from assorted scraps.

Cut out appliqués, adding 1/4" seam allowance around each piece.

2. Sew one Fabric E Wedge 2 between one regular and one reverse Fabric D Wedge 1. Stop and anchor stitching 1/4" from outside edge. Press seams open. Make thirty-six.

Make 36

3. Sew one Fabric F plate point between two units from step 2. Stop and anchor stitching 1/4" from outside edge. Press seams open. Make eighteen.

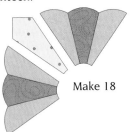

Make 18

4. Arrange and sew two units from step 3 and two Fabric F plate points as shown. Stop and anchor stitching 1/4" from outside edge. Press seams open. Make nine.

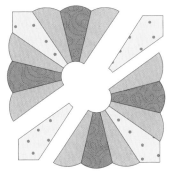

Make 9

5. Refer to quilt layout on page 36 and color photo on page 39. Center and pin one Dresden Plate to alternating Fabric A background squares as shown. Use preferred method to hand appliqué Dresden Plates and center circles in place.

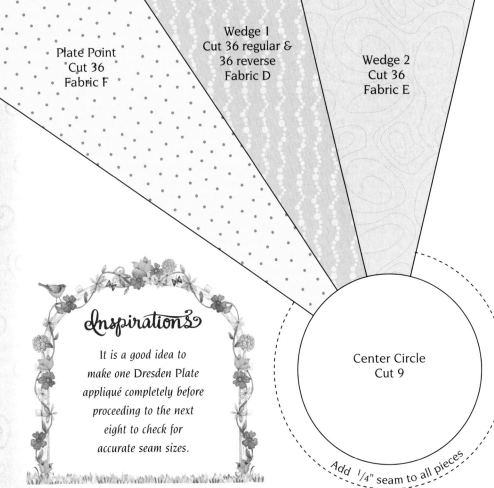

Plate Point
Cut 36
Fabric F

Wedge 1
Cut 36 regular &
36 reverse
Fabric D

Wedge 2
Cut 36
Fabric E

Center Circle
Cut 9

Add 1/4" seam to all pieces

*Inspirations*

*It is a good idea to make one Dresden Plate appliqué completely before proceeding to the next eight to check for accurate seam sizes.*

## Borders

1. Sew 1½" x 42" accent border strips end to end to make one continuous 1½"-wide strip. Refer to Adding the Borders on page 80. Measure quilt through center from side to side. Trim two 1½"-wide accent border strips to that measurement. Sew to top and bottom. Press seams toward accent borders.

2. Measure quilt through center from top to bottom, including borders just added. Trim two 1½"-wide accent border strips to that measurement. Sew to sides and press.

3. Repeat steps 1 and 2 to join, fit, trim, and sew 2"-wide middle border strips to top, bottom, and sides of quilt. Press seams toward middle borders.

4. Repeat steps 1 and 2 to join, fit, trim, and sew 3½"-wide outside border strips to top, bottom, and sides of quilt. Press seams toward outside borders.

## Layering and Finishing

1. Cut backing crosswise into two equal pieces. Sew pieces together to make one 78" x 82" (approximate) backing piece. Cut backing to 78" x 78". Arrange and baste backing, batting, and top together referring to Layering the Quilt directions on page 80.

2. Hand or machine quilt. Use background color or contrasting thread to quilt Dresden Plate motif in alternate Fabric A background squares.

3. Sew 2¾" x 42" binding strips together in pairs. Refer to Binding the Quilt directions on page 80 and bind quilt to finish.

# GARDEN TEA PARTY

*Beautiful and delicious, these tea party treats are made with quick and easy cooking techniques so you can enjoy the party as much as your guests! We created an edible centerpiece by using a tiered tray and placing the croissants on the bottom tier, tarts on the middle tier, and a small flower arrangement on the top tier. Garnish each tier with mint and fresh edible pansies for a delectable and adorable centerpiece! Stacked glass cake plates would work just as well as our tiered tray. We added mini scones, berry preserves, and fresh fruit for a colorful and delicious display.*

### Sierra Chicken Croissants

1½ cups chopped & cooked chicken breasts
¾ cup diced celery
½ cup quartered seedless red grapes
¼ cup toasted pecans*
Purchased creamy honey mustard dressing
Cheddar cheese slices
12 mini croissants
Lettuce

Mix first four ingredients and then add dressing to moisten the mixture. Slice mini croissants and brush with a little dressing, add Sierra Chicken mixture, a slice of cheddar cheese, and crisp lettuce. Store in refrigerator until ready to serve.

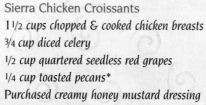

*To toast pecans, place pecans in a dry frying pan and toast stirring constantly over medium heat.

### Jeweled Fruit Tarts
#### Pie Dough

This recipe will make a covered 9" pie, two shells, or approximately 50 small tart shells.

3 cups flour
1 teaspoon salt
1⅓ cups butter flavored shortening

Mix the flour and salt together and then cut in the shortening.

Mix together:
1 egg, beaten with a fork
1 tablespoon vinegar
5 tablespoons cold water

Add egg mixture to flour mixture using a fork, then knead dough until it becomes smooth. Roll out part of the dough at a time.

Cut with scalloped-edge cookie cutter. Press into mini tart pans. Use a fork to prick the dough and then sprinkle with sugar. Place on a cookie sheet and bake until golden brown in pre-heated 425 degree oven for 8-10 minutes, watching carefully. Cool. Remove from tart pans and fill with chilled Easy Chantilly Cream.

### Easy Chantilly Cream

1 box instant vanilla pudding mixed with only 1 cup of milk and chilled until firm.
1 cup whipping cream, whipped with vanilla, powdered sugar, and a dash of salt to taste.

Gently fold the pudding and the flavored whipped cream together. Chill for about 15 minutes before filling tart shells. Top each tart with your choice of fruit. Sliced strawberries, halved grapes, Mandarin orange slices, kiwi, and berries are all good choices. Brush the finished tart with slightly cooled glaze.

### Glaze

⅔ cup apple jelly (or any clear jelly)
1 tablespoon sugar.

Mix together in a saucepan and melt over low heat. Cool slightly before brushing onto decorated tarts.

Recipes were provided by:
Catered Ambiance
1104 W. Wellesley Avenue
Spokane, Washington 99205

"I will be the gladdest thing *under the sun!*
I will touch a hundred *flowers* and not pick one."

~ Edna St. Vincent Millay, "Afternoon on a Hill"

Garlands of color encircle
a glorious garden mum,
While a kaleidoscope of patterns
becomes flowery fields.
And a window holds the key
to year-round blooms
As summertime to Autumn yields.

"*Flowers leave some of their fragrance in the hand that bestows them.*"

~ *Chinese Proverb*

### A Natural Focal Point!

The glorious appliqués and garlands of diamonds make this quilt a natural to be a focal point on your wall.

Hang it on an appropriately sized wall where it can be seen from a distance. Highlight that wall with a different paint color from the rest of the room to make your Mumm Medallion Lap Quilt stand out even more.

Or drape it over a wicker chair or settee for a charming accent to your home.

# Mumm Medallion
## Lap Quilt

**Mumm Medallion Lap Quilt**
*Finished size 56" square*
*Photo page 47*

*You'll be charmed by the single oversize blossom beaming from the center of this sunny medallion lap quilt. Surrounded by "garlands" of simple pieced blocks and graceful, trailing appliqués, this fantasy flower heralds the onset of autumn.*

# Fabric Requirements and Cutting Instructions

Read all instructions before beginning and use 1/4"-wide seam allowances throughout. Read Cutting the Strips and Pieces on page 78 prior to cutting fabrics.

| | | First Cut | | Second Cut | |
|---|---|---|---|---|---|
| | | Number of Strips or Pieces | Dimensions | Number of Pieces | Dimensions |
| ▢ | Fabric A Background 1 1/6 yards | 1 | 17 1/2" square | | |
| | | 4 | 5 1/2" x 42" | 2 | 5 1/2" x 31 1/2" |
| | | | | 2 | 5 1/2" x 41 1/2" |
| ▨ | Fabric B Block Centers 1/8 yard of seven fabrics 1/4 yard of two fabrics | 72 | 4 1/2" squares | | |
| ▤ | Fabric C Inside Block 1 Triangles 1/2 yard | 6 | 2 1/2" x 42" | 96 | 2 1/2" squares |
| ▨ | Fabric D Outside Block 2 Triangles 1 yard | 12 | 2 1/2" x 42" | 192 | 2 1/2" squares |
| ◉ | Ruched Flowers 1/8 yard each of seven different fabrics | 2 | 2" x 42" *(for center ruched flower)* | | |
| | | 1 | 2" x 42" *(for each of six fabrics)* | | |
| **Borders** | | | | | |
| ▧ | Fabric E Inside Block 1 Borders 1/2 yard | 6 | 2" x 42" | 2 | 2" x 17 1/2" |
| | | | | 2 | 2" x 20 1/2" |
| | | | | 2 | 2" x 28 1/2" |
| | | | | 2 | 2" x 31 1/2" |
| ▨ | Fabric F Outside Block 2 Borders 2/3 yard | 10 | 2" x 42" | | |
| ▨ | Binding 1/2 yard | 6 | 2 3/4" x 42" | | |

Appliqués (flower petals, veins, and leaves) - scraps
Backing - 3 5/8 yards
Batting - 63" x 63"
Template Plastic, Optional

## Preparing the Medallion Block

Refer to Hand Appliqué directions on page 79. If you prefer the quick-fuse appliqué method, be sure to reverse all appliqué templates and refer to Quick-Fuse Appliqué directions on page 78.

1. Trace appliqué designs from pages 48-49. Make templates and use assorted scraps to trace eight each of pieces 1 and 2 (leaves and leaf veins) and four each of pieces 3-10 (flower petals). Cut out appliques, adding 1/4" seam allowance around each piece. Ruched flower center will be added after quilting.

2. Fold 17 1/2" Fabric A square in half vertically, horizontally, and diagonally, and press lightly to find centerpoint. Refer to placement diagram on page 48 and position appliqués on Fabric A square. Hand appliqué leaves, leaf veins, and flower petals in place.

### Helpful Hint

Accurate seam allowances are always important, but especially so when the quilt top contains multiple pieced borders with lots of blocks—and seams! If each seam is off as little as 1/16", you'll soon find yourself struggling with components that just won't fit. To ensure you are stitching a perfect 1/4"-wide seam, try this simple test. Cut three strips of fabric, each exactly 1 1/2" x 12". With right sides together, and long raw edges aligned, sew two strips together, carefully maintaining a 1/4" seam. Press. Add the third strip to complete the strip set. Press and measure. The finished strip set should measure 3 1/2" x 12". The center strip should measure 1"-wide, the two outside strips 1 1/4"-wide, and the seam allowances exactly 1/4". If your measurements differ, check to make sure that you have pressed the seams flat. If your strip set still doesn't "measure up," try stitching a new strip set, adjusting the seam allowance until you are able to achieve a perfect 1/4"-wide seam.

## Making the Blocks

This quilt requires two different color block variations. You will be making 24 of Block 1 (Fabric C triangles) and 48 of Block 2 (Fabric D triangles).

**1.** Refer to Quick Corner Triangle directions on page 78. For each block, sew two 2¹/₂" Fabric C squares to opposite corners of a 4¹/₂" Fabric B square. Press. Repeat to sew two 2¹/₂" Fabric C squares to remaining two corners of each unit. Press. Make twenty-four. Label these Block 1. Block measures 4¹/₂".

Note: if you are using striped fabric, carefully position each square, and then check before stitching to make sure stripes will lie in correct direction.

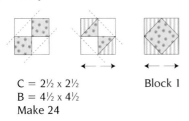

C = 2½ x 2½
B = 4½ x 4½
Make 24                    Block 1

**2.** Refer to Quick Corner Triangle directions on page 78. For each block, sew two 2¹/₂" Fabric D squares to opposite corners of a 4¹/₂" Fabric B square. Press. Repeat to sew two 2¹/₂" Fabric D squares to remaining two corners of each unit. Press. Make forty-eight. Label these Block 2. Block measures 4¹/₂".

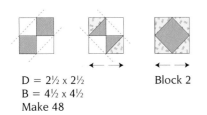

D = 2½ x 2½
B = 4½ x 4½
Make 48                    Block 2

## Assembly

**1.** Sew 2" x 17¹/₂" Fabric E strips to top and bottom of appliquéd medallion block. Press seams toward border. Sew 2" x 20¹/₂" Fabric E strips to sides of block. Press.

**2.** Sew five of Block 1 together to make a strip. Press seams open. Pieced strip measures 4¹/₂" x 20¹/₂". Make two strips. Repeat to make two seven-block strips. Press seams open. Pieced strip measures 4¹/₂" x 28¹/₂".

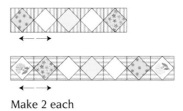

Make 2 each

**3.** Sew a five-block pieced strip from step 2 to top and bottom of bordered medallion block. Press seams toward inside border. Repeat to sew seven-block pieced strips to sides of block. Press.

**4.** Sew 2" x 28¹/₂" Fabric E strips to top and bottom. Press seams toward border. Sew 2" x 31¹/₂" Fabric E strips to sides. Press.

**5.** Sew 5¹/₂" x 31¹/₂" Fabric A strips to top and bottom. Press seams toward Fabric E strips. Sew 5¹/₂" x 41¹/₂" Fabric A strips to sides. Press.

**6.** Cut two 2"-wide Fabric F strips to 2" x 41¹/₂". Sew to top and bottom. Press seams toward narrow border.

**7.** Sew remaining 2" x 42" Fabric F strips end to end to make one continuous 2"-wide strip. Cut two 2" x 44¹/₂" Fabric F strips to that measurement. Sew to sides. Press.

**8.** Sew eleven of Block 2 together to make a strip. Press seams open. Pieced strip measures 4¹/₂" x 44¹/₂". Make two strips. Repeat to make two thirteen-block strips. Pieced strip measures 4¹/₂" x 52¹/₂".

Make 2 each

**9.** Sew an eleven-block pieced strip from step 8 to top and bottom of quilt. Press seams toward narrow border. Repeat to sew two thirteen-block pieced strips to sides of quilt. Press.

**10.** Using remaining 2"-wide Fabric F strips, cut two pieces 2" x 52¹/₂" and two pieces 2" x 55¹/₂". Sew 2"-wide border strips to top, bottom, and sides of quilt. Press toward narrow border.

## Appliquéing the Borders

**1.** Trace appliqué designs from pages 48-49. Make templates and use assorted scraps to trace four (two regular and two reversed) each of pieces 12 and 16 (stems); 13, 15, 17, 19, and 21 (leaves); and 14, 18, and 20 (leaf veins). Cut out appliqués, adding ¹/₄" seam allowance around each piece.

**2.** Refer to quilt layout on page 44 and position appliques on Fabric A borders. Use preferred method to hand appliqué stems, leaves, and leaf veins in place. Ruched flowers will be added after quilting.

**3.** To make flower, coil three of the petal shapes to form the center. Secure in place. Continue coiling around until the flower is desired size, securing and tucking under raw ends. Refer to quilt layout on page 44 and stitch flowers to quilt.

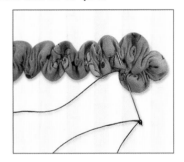

**4.** Divide two 2¾" x 42" binding strips in half, and sew one half to each remaining 2¾"-wide binding strip. Refer to Binding the Quilt directions on page 80 and bind quilt to finish.

## Layering and Finishing

**1.** Cut backing crosswise into two equal pieces. Sew the pieces together to make one 65" x 82" (approximate) backing piece. Cut backing to 63" square. Arrange and baste backing, batting, and top together referring to Layering the Quilt directions on page 80.

**2.** Hand or machine quilt as desired.

## Ruched Flowers and Binding

Note: Use 2" x 42" strips for side flowers. Use 2" x 60" strip for center flower.

**1.** To make flowers, place fabric right side down, fold raw edges of 2"-wide ruched flower strip lengthwise to meet raw edges at center. Press. Fold in half lengthwise and press. Strip should measure ½"-wide.

With pencil, mark bottom edge at 1" intervals. Mark top edge at 1" intervals starting ½" from end.

double fold

single fold

**2.** Beginning at the top, hand-baste from top mark to bottom mark and back to the next top mark forming a zigzag pattern. Make stitches approximately ⅛" long. Gently pull thread tight, gathering fabric to approximately one-third of original size, forming a row of petal-like shapes. Knot end.

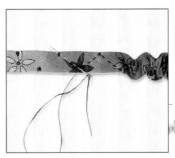

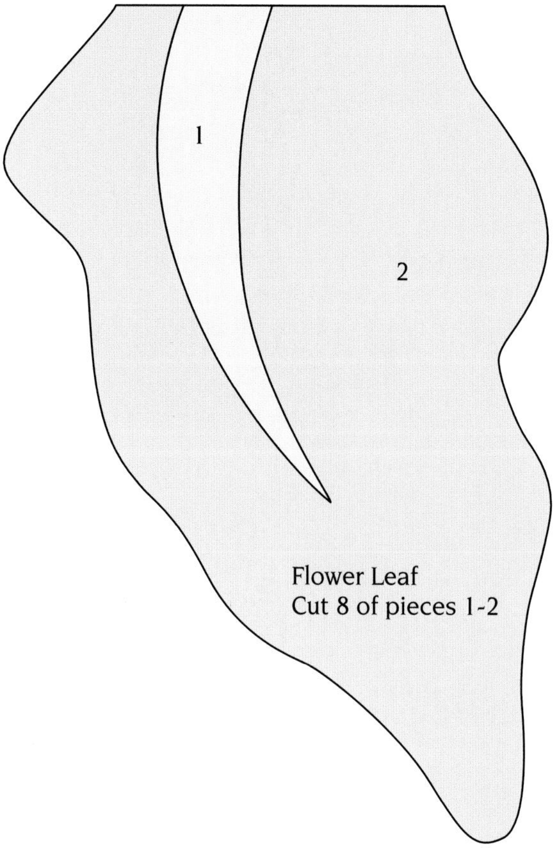

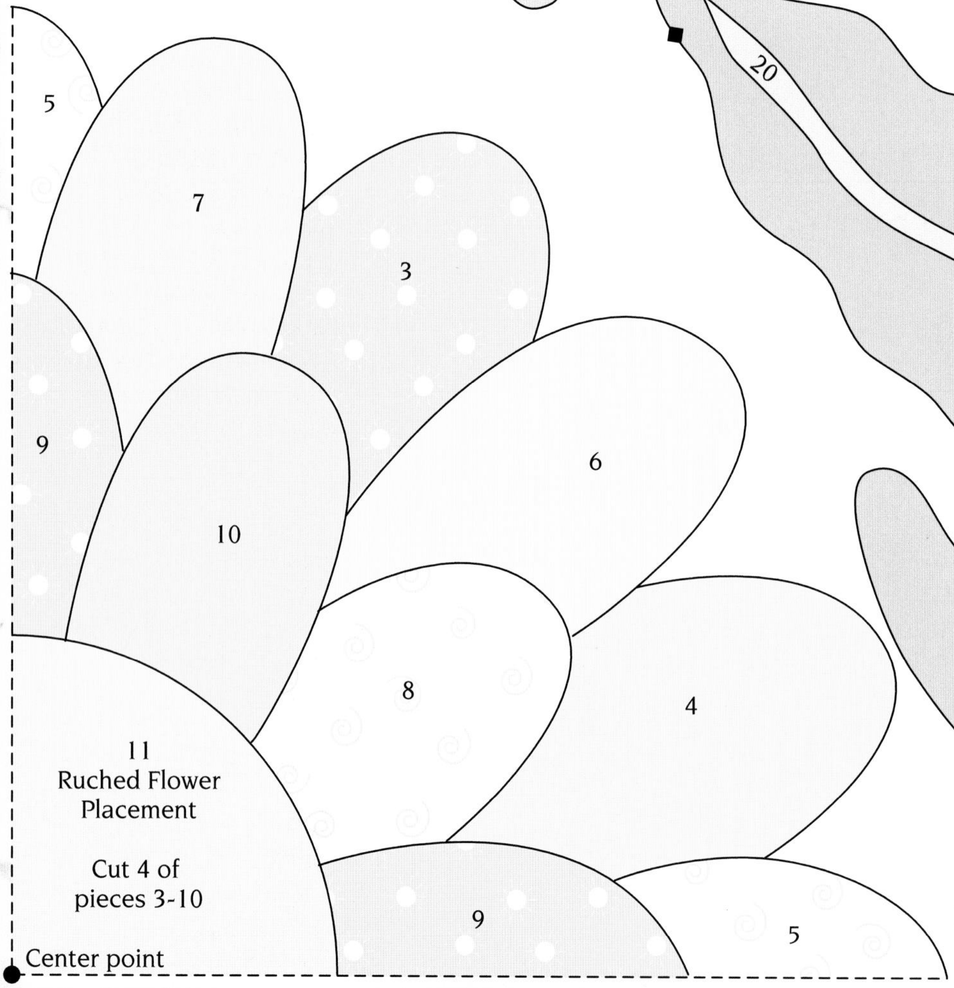

1

2

Flower Leaf
Cut 8 of pieces 1-2

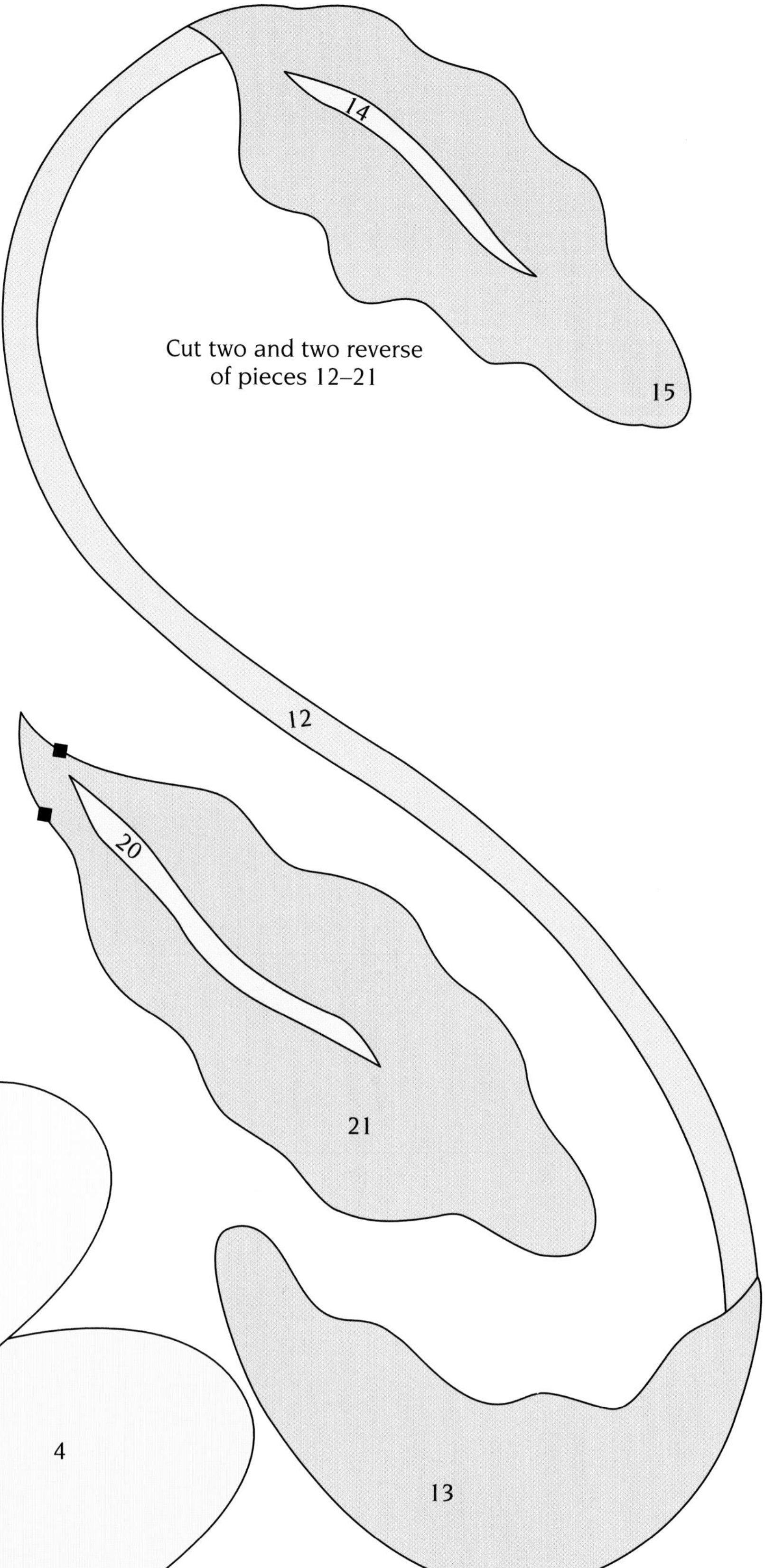

Cut two and two reverse
of pieces 12–21

14

15

12

20

21

13

5

7

3

9

6

10

8

4

11
Ruched Flower
Placement

Cut 4 of
pieces 3-10

9

5

Center point

Placement diagram

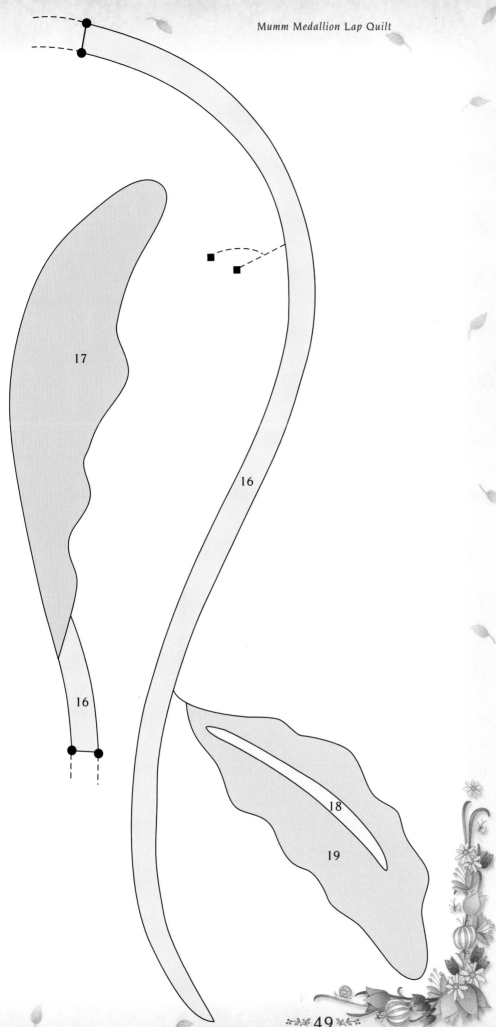

# MEDALLION PILLOW

*24" square*
*Photo: page 47*

Fabric A - ½ *yard*
Accent Border - ⅛ *yard*
Outside Border - ⅓ *yard*
Lining & Batting - 26" x 26"
Backing - ¾ *yard*

**1.** *Sew 1½" x 17½" accent border to top and bottom of 17½" Fabric A square. Press.*

**2.** *Sew 1½" x 19½" accent border to sides. Press.*

**3.** *Repeat steps 1 and 2 to sew 3" x 19½" outside border strips to top and bottom. Sew 3" x 24½" to sides of pillow. Press.*

**4.** *Refer to Quick-Fuse Appliqué directions on page 78. Use reverse image of Medallion Quilt Appliqué patterns on page 48. Fuse appliqués in place and finish with decorative machine or hand stitching as desired.*

## Finishing the Pillow

*Refer to Finishing the Pillow instructions on page 70, replacing the 23½" x 14½" backing pieces with 24½" x 15" backing pieces. Overlap back panels to make 24" square.*

*Option 1: Make a 17" finished pillow form following instructions on page 70. Stitch in the seam between Fabric A and accent border of finished Medallion Pillow to form a flange.*

*Option 2: Purchase a 24" pillow form to insert into pillow.*

# FLORAL KALEIDOSCOPE
### Bed Quilt

**Floral Kaleidoscope Bed Quilt**
*Finished Size: 76³/4" x 95¹/2"*
*Photo: page 53*

*If you've ever been captivated by the ever-changing images of a child's kaleidoscope, you'll love this intriguing fabric interpretation. Although base on just two colorways of one fabric, each flower is a mystery until it's stitched together ... and the variations are amazing! Construction is no mystery, though. The trick is in how the fabrics are layered and cut.*

---

*"My garden of flowers is also my garden of thoughts and dreams."*

~Abram L. Urban

### Complementing your quilt!

The beautiful color blend of the Floral Kaleidoscope Bed Quilt is at once rich and subtle, so keep accessories simple. Select a single color, complementary to your border print, to use for a bed skirt and pillow shams. Soft sponging in a slightly lighter or darker color than your basecoat will help your walls echo the subtle richness of your quilt. Repeating the hexagonal shape of the flower centers in a mirror or other accessories will reinforce the kaleidoscope theme and draw even more attention to the centerpiece of your room!

## Fabric Requirements and Cutting Instructions

Be sure to read Cutting and Layering Panels for Flower Centers before proceeding to cut Fabrics A and B. Also, read Cutting the Strips and Pieces on page 78 for guidance in cutting remainder of fabric strips. Read all instructions before beginning and use 1/4"-wide seam allowances throughout.

| | First Cut | |
| --- | --- | --- |
| | Number of Strips or Pieces | Dimensions |
| Fabric A Flower Center Panels 4 yards* | 4 | 41/2" x 22"** |
| Fabric B Flower Center Panels 4 yards* | 3 | 41/2" x 22"** |
| Fabric C Flower Points 1/2 yard each of 5 different colors | 3 | 41/2" x 42" |
| Fabric D Background 21/4 yards | 17 | 41/2" x 42" |
| **Borders** | | |
| Accent Border 1/2 yard | 8 | 11/2" x 42" |
| Outside Border 13/8 yards Note: you will have enough extra of either Fabric A or B to use as the border if desired. | 8 | 51/2" x 42" |
| Binding 7/8 yard | 9 | 23/4" x 42" |

Backing - 53/4 yards
Batting - 83" x 102"
Rotary ruler w/ 60-degree mark, mat & cutter

*This yardage was based upon fabrics with a pattern that repeats every 12".
Your yardage will vary depending upon the fabric you choose.
Read Cutting and Layering the Panels to determine precise yardage required for your particular fabric.
**Cut strips after layering and aligning fabrics (see steps 1–3.)

## Cutting and Layering Panels for Flower Centers

Flower Centers are formed using a cutting technique developed by Bethany S. Reynolds and detailed in her book, *Magic Stack-n-Whack™ Quilts* (AQS 1998). Fabric panels are stacked, matching motifs, then cut. We used two colorways of the same fabric for our panels. Each panel should measure 22" wide. This allows for some extra fabric.

1. Determine how often the print pattern repeats. You'll want to work with a panel that measures at least 20" long. If repeat is smaller, use multiple repeats until total surpasses 20". In our sample, the pattern repeated every 12", so we figured on 24"—or two repeats—for each panel. For determining yardage see "Inspirations" below.

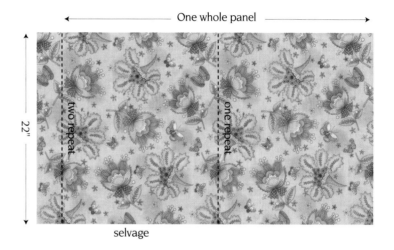

← One whole panel →
22"
two repeat
one repeat
selvage

2. Measure 22" from selvage across Fabric A. Make a clip in top edge of yardage, and divide it by tearing a 22"-wide strip down entire length. Set one piece of fabric aside for outside border, backing, or for another project.

3. Divide 22"-wide length of Fabric A into six panels equal in length to the repeat determined in Step 1 (e.g., six 22" x 24" panels in our sample).

## Inspirations

To determine overall yardage required for specific fabric, multiply repeat determined in Step 1 by 6 (e.g., 24" x 6 = 144" or 4 yards each for Fabrics A & B).

4. Repeat steps 1 through 3 with Fabric B.

5. Layer all six panels of Fabric A right side up on your cutting mat, with selvage and all raw edges carefully matched. Choose a prominent, easily distinguishable element in one motif. Insert point of a flat flower pin directly through this exact spot in the motif.

6. Lift one layer of fabric and carefully reinsert same pin to mark exact same spot of motif on fabric layer below. Continue lifting and pinning, catching one layer at a time, until pin pierces and aligns all six layers. Secure pin.

7. Move across surface of panel, picking another distinguishable element in a motif, and repeating steps 5 and 6. Continue until entire fabric is carefully aligned and securely pinned (approximately every 3"- 4").

8. Repeat steps 5 through 7 with Fabric B.

## Making Flower Centers

You'll be making a total of thirty-eight complete flower centers: twenty-one from Fabric A, and seventeen from Fabric B. Finger press bias seams open as each flower center is assembled. Press with an iron when unit is complete (step 7).

1. Using rotary cutter, cut pinned fabrics into 4½" x 22" strips as shown. Take care not to cut over pins.

4½

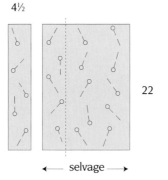

22

← selvage →

2. Using rotary cutter and 60-degree mark on rotary ruler, cut one end of one layered set of 4½" x 22" Fabric A strips at 60-degree angle as shown. Cut 4½" diamonds aligning the ruler to previous cut edge. Repeat to cut eleven stacks of Fabric A diamonds.

60° angle

3. Working one stack of diamonds at a time, cut diamonds across width as shown. Immediately pin each resulting triangle stack along outside straight of grain edge. Be sure to keep each set of six identical (layered) triangles pinned together. One set of triangles will make one flower center.

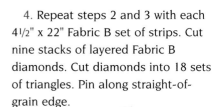

4. Repeat steps 2 and 3 with each 4½" x 22" Fabric B set of strips. Cut nine stacks of layered Fabric B diamonds. Cut diamonds into 18 sets of triangles. Pin along straight-of-grain edge.

*Inspirations*

*For best results with this technique, use flat flower head pins. The flat heads do not cause "humps," or otherwise distort the fabric, as you are pinning and rotary cutting. Pins will not need to be removed unless they are in direct line of the rotary cutter.*

5. Working one stack of triangles at a time, pin outside straight of grain edge for each triangle piece in the stack. Sew two identical triangles together, making sure straight of grain (pinned) edges are positioned as shown. Finger press seams open. Make two identical units.

Make 2

6. Add a third identical triangle to each unit from step 5, once again carefully positioning straight of grain edge. Finger press. Make two.

Make 2

7. Sew two identical units from step 6 together, carefully pinning center to match seams. Press finished unit. Make only one flower center at a time. Make twenty-one.

Make 21 (Fabric A)
Make 17 (Fabric B)

8. Repeat steps 5 through 7 to make seventeen Fabric B flower centers. Press.

9. Repeat step 2 to cut diamonds from each 4 1/2" x 42" Fabric C strip. Cut each diamond into two triangles, marking straight of grain edges with a pin as before. Cut twenty-four diamonds (forty-eight triangles) in each color. You'll have some left over, but you'll have more flexibility in laying out rows.

Row Layout

Row 1
Row 2
Row 3
Row 4
Row 5
Row 6
Row 7
Row 8
Row 9
Row 10
Row 11
Row 12
Row 13
Row 14
Row 15

## Inspirations

*Stitching the rows is simple straight-seam sewing. The challenge is in keeping track of color placement and straight of grain. Use a design wall to lay out rows. Work on one row at a time, repositioning units as soon as they are sewn. This procedure will make keeping track of color placement simple, too!*

### Assembling the Rows

1. Sew eighteen Fabric A and fourteen Fabric B flower centers between two matching Fabric C triangles. Make sure straight of grain (pinned) edges are positioned as shown. Finger press seams open.

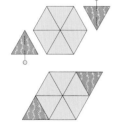

Make 18 (Fabric A)
Make 14 (Fabric B)

2. Repeat steps 1 and 2 of Making Flower Centers to cut diamonds and then triangles, from each 4½" x 42" Fabric D strip. Cut two hundred fifty Fabric D triangles.

3. Referring to Row Layout on page 54, arrange units from step 1 on your design wall, alternating Fabric A and Fabric B units as shown. Continue arranging each flower with Fabric C flower points. Fill in spaces between flowers and flower points with Fabric D background triangles as shown. Place two Fabric D triangles on each end of rows 2, 6, 10, and 14.

4. Referring to Row 2 on row layout, and diagram from step 7 below, sew Fabric C and Fabric D triangles between flowers together in pairs, making sure straight of grain (pinned) edges are positioned as shown. Finger press. Make eight.

Make 8 to match flower points          Make 8 to match flower points

5. Sew units from step 4 together in pairs. Finger press. Make four for row 2.

Make 4

6. Refer to row 2 in layout. Sew Fabric C and Fabric D triangles together in pairs, making sure straight of grain (pinned) edges are positioned as shown. Finger press. Make one each. Sew one Fabric D triangle as shown to complete each unit. Press.

Make 1 to match flower points          Make 1 to match flower points

7. Sew units from steps 1, 5, and 6 together to complete Row 2. Press.

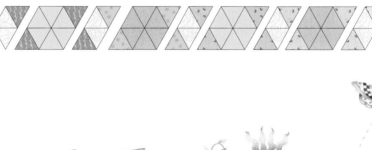

8. Refer to row layout on page 54. Repeat steps 4 through 7 to arrange and sew Rows 6, 10, and 14. Position completed rows on your design wall.

9. Sew Fabric D triangles together in pairs, making sure straight of grain (pinned) edges are positioned as shown. Finger press. Make eighty.

Make 80

10. Row 3 layout on page 54 consists of ten units from step 9, five Fabric C triangles to match flowers in row 2 above, and six assorted Fabric C triangles to match row 4 below.

11. Sew one Fabric C triangle and one unit from step 9 together. Finger press. Make five each.

Make 5 each to match flower points

12. Sew units from step 11 and remaining Fabric C triangle together to complete row 3. Press.

13. Refer to row layout on page 54. Repeat steps 11 and 12 to sew rows 5, 7, 9, 11, and 13, taking care to match Fabric C flower points to adjacent rows. Position completed rows on your design wall.

14. Refer to row 4 on row layout on page 54. Repeat steps 4 and 5 to sew Fabric C and Fabric D triangles together. You'll be making ten pairs of triangles (step 4) and five complete units (step 5). Finger press. Continue to complete rows 8 and 12 taking care to match Fabric C flower points to adjacent rows. Position completed rows on your design wall.

15. To make row 1, sew Fabric C and D triangles together in pairs as shown. Finger press. Make five.

Make 5 to match
flower points

16. Refer to Row Layout on page 54. Arrange and sew ten Fabric D units from step 9, five units from step 15, and one Fabric D triangle to make row 1, taking care to match Fabric C flower points to adjacent row. Press. Position completed row on design wall.

17. Refer to row layout on page 54. Repeat steps 15 and 16 to arrange and sew row 15. Position completed rows on your design wall.

Note: Due to cutting process, in addition to Fabric C triangles, you'll have a few Fabric A and B triangles left over as well. You can set these aside for another project.

## Assembly

1. Refer to Row Layout on page 54 to check that rows 1 through 15 are arranged as shown. Be sure rows are positioned so each flower center is surrounded by six same-color Fabric C triangles.

2. Sew rows together. Press. Square off sides of quilt top by trimming end triangles as shown, making sure to leave ¼"-wide seam allowance.

Cut Line     ------
Seam Line   ············

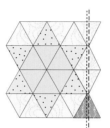

Trim
Leave ¼"-wide
seam allowance

3. Sew 1½" x 42" accent border strips end to end to make one continuous 1½"-wide strip. Referring to Adding the Borders on page 80, measure quilt through center from side to side. Cut two 1½"-wide inside border strips to that measurement. Sew to top and bottom. Press seams toward inside border.

4. Measure quilt through center from top to bottom, including borders just added. Cut two 1½"-wide inside border strips to that measurement. Sew to sides. Press.

5. Repeat steps 3 and 4 to join, fit, trim, and sew 5½" outside border strips to top, bottom, and sides. Press.

## Layering and Finishing

1. Cut backing crosswise into two equal pieces. Sew the pieces together to make one 82" x 103" (approximate) backing piece. Arrange and baste backing, batting, and top together referring to Layering the Quilt directions on page 80.

2. Hand or machine quilt as desired.

3. Sew 2¾" x 42" binding strips together to make four pairs. Divide remaining 2¾" x 42" binding strips in half, and sew one half to two pieced 2¾"-wide binding strips. Refer to Binding the Quilt directions on page 80 and bind quilt to finish. Use shorter strips for top and bottom, and longer strips for sides.

# WILDFLOWER WINDOW
## Pressed Flower Display

**Wildflower Window**

### Add Charm with Pressed Flowers

Bring the sunny glow of flowers to your home year-round! Pressed flowers are a wonderful way to add color and charm to every room. Try placing them under a piece of glass on a coffee table or end table. Make a charming picture for your wall by framing your pressed flower arrangement. Paint a wooden tray then decorate with pressed flowers, placing a piece of glass over the top. Pressed flowers can also be used to decorate cards, scrapbook pages, candles, coasters, place cards, the list is endless!

*The flower-filled beauty of a mountain meadow will be easy to remember when you make this wildflower window for your home. A vintage window frames our wildflower sampler and beautiful lettering identifies each flower. This window and other pressed flower projects are easy to do with materials you have on hand. We pressed our flowers in a telephone book and used a computer for the lettering! This is a great way to preserve and identify those glorious wildflowers of summer!*

## Materials Needed

Fresh flowers
Telephone book or flower press
Window with wooden mullions
Acrylic paints in ivory and
    medium green
Crackle Medium
Translucent paper
White glue
Tweezers
Tooth picks
Indoor Use:
Non-fusible double sided adhesive
Outdoor Use:
Backing glass
Glazing points
Clear silicone sealant

## Pressing Flowers

Hobby stores offer a variety of flower presses including ones that can be used in microwave ovens. Flower presses are also easy to make using peg board, blotter paper, and screws with wing nuts. Look for directions on how to make a flower press on the Internet or in hobby books. We pressed most of our flowers by carefully positioning them in old telephone books. It took a little longer for flowers to thoroughly dry, but the results were excellent. We left our flowers in the telephone book for one week. If you live in an area with high humidity, it may take longer. Flowers will be brittle when they are thoroughly dried.

## Preparing the Window

**1.** Lightly sand all wood surfaces and thoroughly wash window. Allow to dry.

**2.** Using acrylic paints, base coat the window frame with ivory paint. Dry thoroughly.

**3.** Apply crackle medium to window frame and allow to set according to manufacturer's directions.

**4.** Apply a quick, even coat of medium green paint to window frame. Crackle will appear in freshly painted surface. Do not touch, as surface is very fragile when wet. Dry thoroughly.

**5.** Apply a coat of matte varnish to painted surface.

**6.** Scrape all paint from windowpanes and clean glass thoroughly.

## Decorating the Window

We purchased translucent paper at a scrapbook store for our background and used a wildflower reference book to identify our wildflowers. Using 150 point type in a French Script and a medium gray color, we typed the name of each flower on a computer, positioning the name where we wanted it to appear on the paper.

We then printed the names directly onto the translucent paper using a standard printer, then cut paper to size for window panes. You can hand-letter the names onto the paper, if desired, or if your window panes are too large. You may also want to consider printing the names in a color to match your flowers or your décor.

Indoor Use:

**1.** Apply non-fusible double-sided adhesive to back side of prepared paper, following manufacturer's instructions. Smooth paper carefully onto top of glass, making sure there are no folds or wrinkles in paper. Repeat for other panes.

**2.** Then, using tweezers, position your flowers as desired around the names. Working one flower at a time, apply tiny dots of white craft glue on the backs of petals and stems using toothpicks. Gently pat flowers into place on translucent paper. Allow to dry thoroughly. Flowers and paper will be on top of the glass. Hang as desired inside your home.

Outdoor Use:

For outdoor use, we recommend "sandwiching" the translucent paper with flowers attached between two pieces of glass.

**1.** Using white glue and following the directions in step 2 above, attach flowers to translucent paper. Place paper with attached flowers behind glass of your window.

**2.** Place a second piece of glass behind paper arrangement and set in place using glazing points. Use clear silicone sealant to seal all sides.

# S·E·R·E·N·I·T·Y

" Bread feeds the *body*, indeed,
but flowers feed also the *soul*. "

-- The Koran

The quiet simplicity of a single
blossom in a bamboo frame,
The subtle intricacy of patterns of thread,
The delicacy of a floral wreath,
Bring quiet contemplation
to your bed.

# TRANQUIL GARDEN
## Bed Quilt

"A garden
is a delight to
the eye and
a solace for
the soul."

*~ Sadi*

### Enhance Quilt Beauty by Repeating Elements

Echo the quiet beauty of our Orient-inspired bed quilt in your bedroom accessories. We constructed a simple wooden headboard to repeat and accentuate the trellis design on the quilt. The wicker-patterned fabric in the quilt is repeated in the bed stand. Several ceramic pieces pick up the color palette and add artful design. Large, graceful plants complement the quiet simplicity of the bedroom setting.

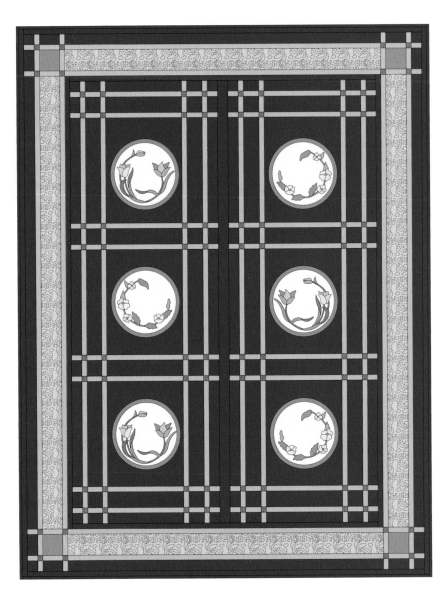

**Tranquil Garden Bed Quilt**
*Finished Size: 81" x 105"*
*Photo: page 60*

*A delicate geometric framework provides a pleasing counterpoint for timeless floral appliqués in this elegantly simple—and simply elegant—Japanese-inspired bed quilt. The result is a serene balance, which belies the deceptively easy, state-of-the-art construction methods.*

# Fabric Requirements and Cutting Instructions

Read all instructions before beginning and use ¼"-wide seam allowances throughout. Read Cutting the Strips and Pieces on page 78 prior to cutting fabrics.

| | First Cut | | Second Cut | |
| | Number of Strips or Pieces | Dimensions | Number of Pieces | Dimensions |
|---|---|---|---|---|
| Fabric A Background *5 yards - fabric must be at least 42" wide* | 3 | 15½" x 42" | 6 | 15½" x 20½" |
| | 1 | 4½" x 42" | | |
| | 13 | 3½" x 42" | | |
| | 20 | 2½" x 42" | 12 | 2½" x 20½" |
| | | | 4 | 2½" x 15½" |
| | | | 12 | 2½" squares |
| | 17 | 1½" x 42" | | |
| Fabric B Trellis *2 ⅜ yards* | 2 | 3½" x 42" | | |
| | 46 | 1½" x 42" | 16 | 1½" x 4½" |
| Fabric C Accent Corners *¼ yard* | 5 | 1½" x 42" | 16 | 1½" squares |
| Fabric D Circle Borders/ Corner Squares *1 yard* | 2 | 14" x 42" | | |
| | 1 | 4½" x 42" | 4 | 4½" squares |
| Fabric E Circle Appliqué Background *¾ yard* | 2 | 12" x 42" | | |
| **Borders** | | | | |
| Accent Border *1 ⅛ yards* | 8 | 4½" x 42" | | |
| Binding *⅞ yard* | 10 | 2¾" x 42" | | |

Appliqués (Flowers, Leaves, and Stems) - assorted scraps
Backing - 8 yards
Batting - 87" x 111"
Lightweight Fusible Web - 2½ yards
Temporary Fabric Spray Adhesive

# Assembling Blocks

**1.** Sew one 3½" x 42" Fabric A strip between two 1½" x 42" Fabric B strips. Repeat to make thirteen 5½" x 42" strip sets. Press toward Fabric B. Using rotary cutter and ruler, cut the following segments from strip sets: twelve 20½" x 5½", eight 15½" x 5½", sixteen 3½" x 5½", and twenty-four 2½" x 5½".

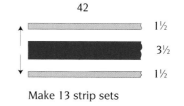

Make 13 strip sets

Cut strips into:

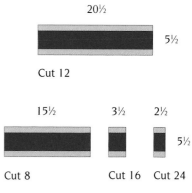

Cut 12

Cut 8    Cut 16    Cut 24

**2.** Sew one 3½" x 42" Fabric B strip between two 1½" x 42" Fabric C strips. Repeat to make two 5½" x 42" strip sets. Press. Cut thirty-two 1½" segments from strip sets.

Make 2 strip sets
Cut 32

**3.** Sew one 3½" x 5½" segment from step 1 between two segments from step 2. Press. Make sixteen.

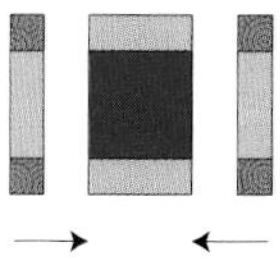

Make 16

**4.** Sew one 15½" x 5½" segment from step 1 between two segments from step 3. Press. Make eight.

15½

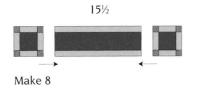

Make 8

**5.** Sew each 15½" x 20½" Fabric A panel between two 20½" x 5½" segments from step 1. Press. Make six.

15½

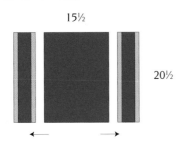

20½

Make 6

**6.** Sew one unit from step 5 between two units from step 4. Press. Make four.

Option: Complete appliqué here if you prefer to work with smaller units.

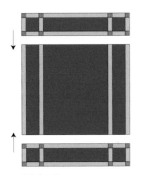

Make 4

**7.** Sew one 2½" x 15½" Fabric A strip between two 2½" x 5½" units from step 1. Press. Make four.

15½

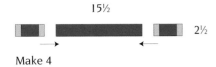

2½

Make 4

**8.** Sew one 2½" x 20½" Fabric A strip between two remaining 2½" x 5½" units from step 1. Press. Make eight. Save for step 10.

20½

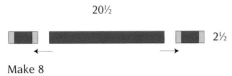

2½

Make 8

**9.** Sew one unit from step 7, one unit from step 6, one unit from step 5, one unit from step 6, and one unit from step 7 to make vertical rows. See Unit A diagram below. Press. Make two.

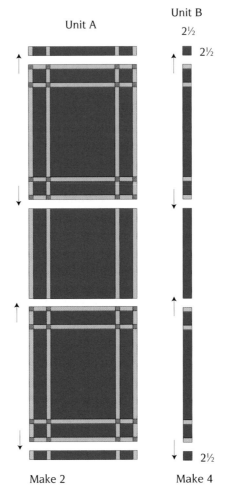

Unit A

Unit B

2½

2½

2½

Make 2        Make 4

**10.** Sew one 2½" Fabric A square, one unit from step 8, one 2½" x 20½" Fabric A strip, one unit from step 8, and one 2½" Fabric A square to make a vertical row as shown. Press. Make four. See Unit B diagram above.

**11.** Sew three 2½" x 42" Fabric A strips end to end to make one continuous 2½"-wide strip. From this strip, cut one 2½" x 84½" strip. Refer to quilt layout on page 62. Arrange one Unit B from step 10, one Unit A from step 9, one Unit B from step 10, 2½" x 84½" Fabric A strip, one Unit B from step 10, one Unit A from step 9, and one Unit B from step 10. Sew rows and units together. Press seams away from Unit A rows.

## Preparing Appliqué Blocks

Refer to Quick-Fuse Appliqué method on page 78. If you prefer traditional hand appliqué, add ¼"-wide seam allowances when cutting appliqué pieces. Refer to Hand Appliqué directions on page 79.

**1.** Trace circle appliqué background pattern on page 76. Cut six from Fabric E. Refer to quilt layout on page 62 and center circle appliqué background on each Unit A panel with temporary fabric spray adhesive.

**2.** Secure circle appliqué backgrounds to panels with machine straight stitch very close to outside edge. To eliminate shadow, carefully trim away Fabric A (blue) background from behind Fabric E circle appliqué background, leaving ¼"-wide seam allowance.

**3.** Refer to Quick-Fuse Appliqué directions on page 78. Trace appliqué circle border pattern on page 76 and flowers, stem, and leaves from pages 66 and 67 to paper-side of fusible web. Trace three (two regular and one reverse) of each appliqué piece.

**4.** Refer to quilt layout on page 62 and position appliqués on each panel. Fuse appliqués in place and finish with a machine satin stitch or decorative stitching as desired.

## Borders

**1.** Sew eight 1½" x 42" Fabric A strips end to end to make one continuous 1½"-wide border strip. Measure quilt through center from side to side. Cut two 1½"-wide border strips to that measurement. Sew to top and bottom. Press seams toward inside border.

**2.** Measure quilt through center from top to bottom, including borders just added. Cut two 1½"-wide border strips to that measurement. Sew to sides. Press.

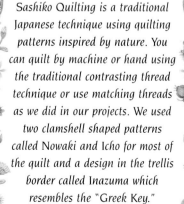

**3.** Sew eight 2¹/₂" x 42" Fabric A strips end to end. Sew eight 1¹/₂" x 42" Fabric B strips end to end. Make two sets. Sew eight 4¹/₂" x 42" accent border strips end to end. Assemble in order shown, staggering seams to make outside border unit.

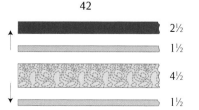

42

2½
1½
4½
1½

**4.** Measure quilt through center from side to side. Cut two 8¹/₂"-wide border units from step 3 to that measurement. Measure quilt through center from top to bottom. Cut two 8¹/₂"-wide border units to that measurement. Sew shorter lengths to top and bottom. Press seams toward border unit. Set remaining border units aside for now.

**5.** Sew one 1¹/₂" x 4¹/₂" Fabric B piece between two 1¹/₂" Fabric C squares. Press. Make eight.

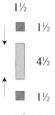

1½
1½
4½
1½

Make 8

**6.** Sew one 4¹/₂" Fabric D square between two 1¹/₂" x 4¹/₂" Fabric B pieces. Press. Make four.

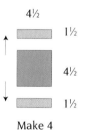

4½
1½
4½
1½

Make 4

**7.** Sew each unit from step 6 between two units from step 5. Press. Make four.

Make 4

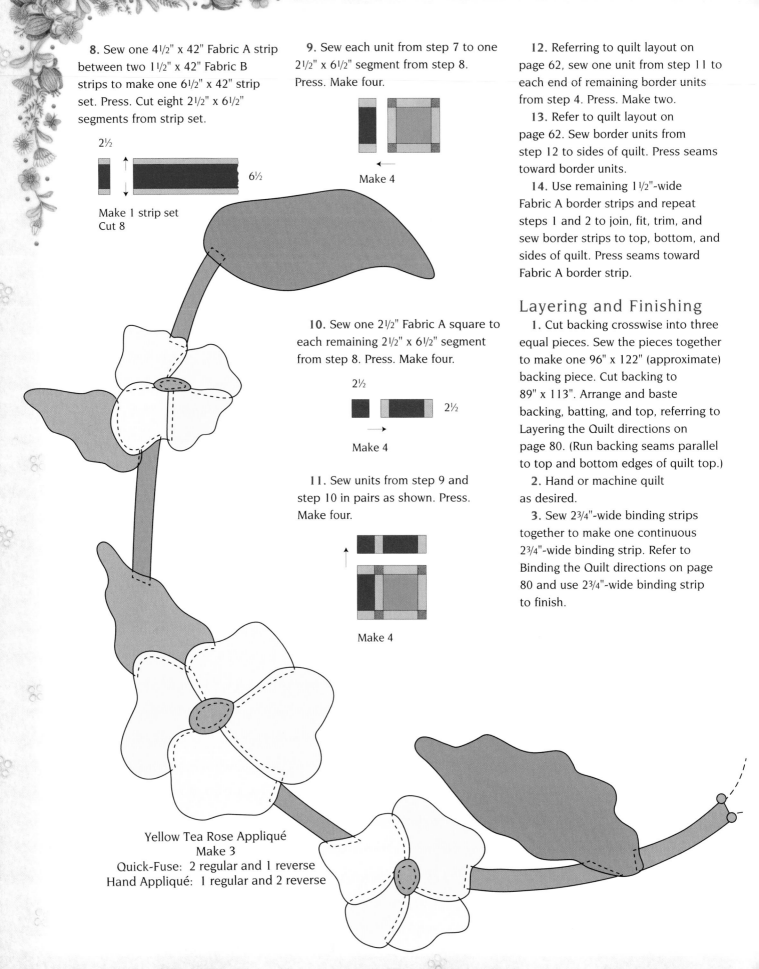

**8.** Sew one 4½" x 42" Fabric A strip between two 1½" x 42" Fabric B strips to make one 6½" x 42" strip set. Press. Cut eight 2½" x 6½" segments from strip set.

2½

6½

Make 1 strip set
Cut 8

**9.** Sew each unit from step 7 to one 2½" x 6½" segment from step 8. Press. Make four.

Make 4

**10.** Sew one 2½" Fabric A square to each remaining 2½" x 6½" segment from step 8. Press. Make four.

2½

2½

Make 4

**11.** Sew units from step 9 and step 10 in pairs as shown. Press. Make four.

Make 4

**12.** Referring to quilt layout on page 62, sew one unit from step 11 to each end of remaining border units from step 4. Press. Make two.

**13.** Refer to quilt layout on page 62. Sew border units from step 12 to sides of quilt. Press seams toward border units.

**14.** Use remaining 1½"-wide Fabric A border strips and repeat steps 1 and 2 to join, fit, trim, and sew border strips to top, bottom, and sides of quilt. Press seams toward Fabric A border strip.

## Layering and Finishing

**1.** Cut backing crosswise into three equal pieces. Sew the pieces together to make one 96" x 122" (approximate) backing piece. Cut backing to 89" x 113". Arrange and baste backing, batting, and top, referring to Layering the Quilt directions on page 80. (Run backing seams parallel to top and bottom edges of quilt top.)

**2.** Hand or machine quilt as desired.

**3.** Sew 2¾"-wide binding strips together to make one continuous 2¾"-wide binding strip. Refer to Binding the Quilt directions on page 80 and use 2¾"-wide binding strip to finish.

Yellow Tea Rose Appliqué
Make 3
Quick-Fuse: 2 regular and 1 reverse
Hand Appliqué: 1 regular and 2 reverse

Tulips Appliqué
Make 3
Quick-Fuse: 2 regular and 1 reverse
Hand Appliqué: 1 regular and 2 reverse

# TRANQUILITY

## *Pillow*

**Tranquility Pillow**
*Finished Size: 17" square*
*(23" square including flange)*
*Photo: page 70*

> "The greatest gift of the garden is the restoration of the five senses."
>
> ~ Hanna Rion

### Sashiko Quilting Adds Style and Interest

Sashiko quilting (page 65) in the flange border on this pillow makes it a small work of art for the bedroom. Stacked on top of a bed pillow as shown in the photograph on page 60 or used on a polished wooden bench, this pillow will add a touch of the Orient to any room. Make a piece of Sashiko Quilting to cover a pre-cut mat then use the mat to frame a simple wood-block print. Hang the framed print low on a wall over a table accessorized with a tea set and Oriental vase. A few branches of crooked willow or a small sampling of seedpods in the vase will add a graceful flourish.

*Whether paired with the elegant bed quilt shown on page 60 or given the spotlight on a favorite sofa or chair, this striking flanged pillow is guaranteed to infuse your décor with a touch of Oriental flair. The instructions are for the single blossom, but if you prefer, you can add the second flower, or adapt an appliqué design from the Tranquil Garden Bed Quilt.*

*Peace*

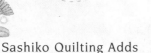

# Fabric Requirements and Cutting Instructions

Read all instructions before beginning and use 1/4"-wide seam allowances throughout. Read Cutting the Strips and Pieces on page 78 prior to cutting fabrics.

| | | First Cut | | Second Cut | |
|---|---|---|---|---|---|
| | | Number of Strips or Pieces | Dimensions | Number of Pieces | Dimensions |
| ▓ | Fabric A Background<br>*3/8 yard* | 1 | 11 1/2" square | | |
| ▒ | Fabric B Circle Border & Trellis Border<br>*1/2 yard* | 1<br>2 | 14" square<br>1 1/2" x 42" | 4<br>8 | 1 1/2" x 11 1/2"<br>1 1/2" x 2 1/2" |
| ▓ | Fabric C Trellis Accent Squares<br>*scraps* | 4 | 1 1/2" squares | | |
| ☐ | Fabric D Circle Appliqué Background<br>*3/8 yard* | 1 | 12" square | | |
| **Borders** | | | | | |
| ▒ | Fabric E Second Border<br>*1/6 yard* | 2 | 2 1/2" x 42" | 4 | 2 1/2" x 11 1/2" |
| ▓ | Fabric F Outside Border<br>*1/4 yard* | 2 | 3 1/2" x 42" | 2<br>2 | 3 1/2" x 17 1/2"<br>3 1/2" x 23 1/2" |
| ▒ | Fabric G Border Corners<br>*scrap* | 4 | 2 1/2" squares | | |
| | Backing<br>*3/4 yard* | 1 | 23 1/2" x 42" | 2 | 23 1/2" x 14 1/2" |

Appliqués (flower, leaf, and stem) - assorted scraps
Lining - 3/4 yard (One 23 1/2" square)
Batting - 23 1/2" square
Lightweight Fusible Web - 3/4 yard
Pillow Form Fabric - 5/8 yard (Two 17 1/2" squares)
Polyester Fiberfill Stuffing
Temporary Fabric Spray Adhesive

# Assembling the Pillow Top

**1.** Sew 11 1/2" Fabric A square between two 1 1/2" x 11 1/2" Fabric B strips. Press.

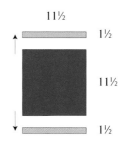

**2.** Sew unit from step 1 between two 2 1/2" x 11 1/2" Fabric E pieces. Press.

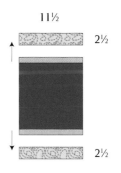

**3.** Sew one 1 1/2" x 2 1/2" Fabric B piece, one 1 1/2" Fabric C square, one 1 1/2" x 11 1/2" Fabric B strip, one 1 1/2" Fabric C square, and one 1 1/2" x 2 1/2" Fabric B piece in order shown. Press. Make two.

Make 2

**4.** Sew one 2 1/2" Fabric G square, one 1 1/2" x 2 1/2" Fabric B piece, one 2 1/2" x 11 1/2" Fabric E piece, one 1 1/2" x 2 1/2" Fabric B piece, and one 2 1/2" Fabric G square in order shown. Press. Make two.

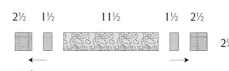

Make 2

**5.** Sew one unit from step 4, one unit from step 3, unit from step 2, one unit from step 3, and one unit from step 4 in order shown. Press.

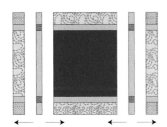

**6.** Sew 3¹/2" x 17¹/2" Fabric F strip to top and bottom of unit. Press.

**7.** Sew 3¹/2" x 23¹/2" Fabric F strip to sides of pillow. Press.

## Preparing the Appliqué

The instructions given are for the Quick-Fuse Appliqué method on page 78. If you prefer traditional hand appliqué, be sure to reverse all appliqué templates, and add 1/4"-wide seam allowances when cutting appliqué pieces. Refer to Hand Appliqué directions on page 79.

**1.** Fold 14" Fabric B square vertically and horizontally into quarters to find center point. Repeat with 12" Fabric D square. Trace appliqué patterns on page 76 to Fabric B for circle border and to Fabric D for circle appliqué background. Refer to pillow layout on page 68. Center circle appliqué background and circle border on pillow top with temporary fabric spray adhesive. Note that appliqués overlap trellis border.

**2.** Secure circle and circle border to pillow top with machine straight stitch, then finish with machine satin stitch or other decorative stitching. To eliminate shadow-through, carefully trim away Fabric A (blue) background from behind Fabric D circle appliqué background, leaving 1/4"-wide seam allowance.

**3.** Refer to Quick-Fuse Appliqué directions on page 78. Trace appliqué patterns for flower and leaf.

**4.** Refer to pillow layout on page 68 and position appliqués on pillow top. Fuse appliqués in place and finish with decorative stitching as desired.

## Finishing the Pillow Cover

**1.** Layer batting between pillow top and lining. Baste. Hand or machine quilt as desired, except for outside border area. Trim batting and lining even with raw edge of pillow top.

**2.** Narrow hem one long edge of each 23¹/2" x 14¹/2" backing piece by folding under 1/4" to wrong side. Fold under 1/4" again to wrong side. Topstitch along folded edge.

**3.** With right sides up, lay one backing piece over second piece so hemmed edges overlap, making single 23¹/2" square backing panel. Baste pieces together at top and bottom where they overlap.

**4.** With right sides together, position and pin pillow top to backing. Using 1/4"-wide seam, sew around edges, trim corners, turn right side out, and press.

**5.** Stitch-in-the-ditch between the second and outside borders to create flange. Add Sashiko-style quilting in flange border.

**6.** Insert pillow form into pillow cover.

## Making Pillow Form

Place 17¹/2" Pillow Form Fabric squares together, aligning raw edges. Using 1/4"-wide seam, sew around all edges, leaving 4" opening for turning. Trim corners and turn right-side out. Stuff to desired fullness with polyester fiberfill and hand stitch opening closed.

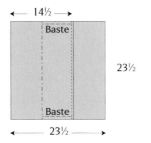

← 14½ →

Baste

23½

Baste

← 23½ →

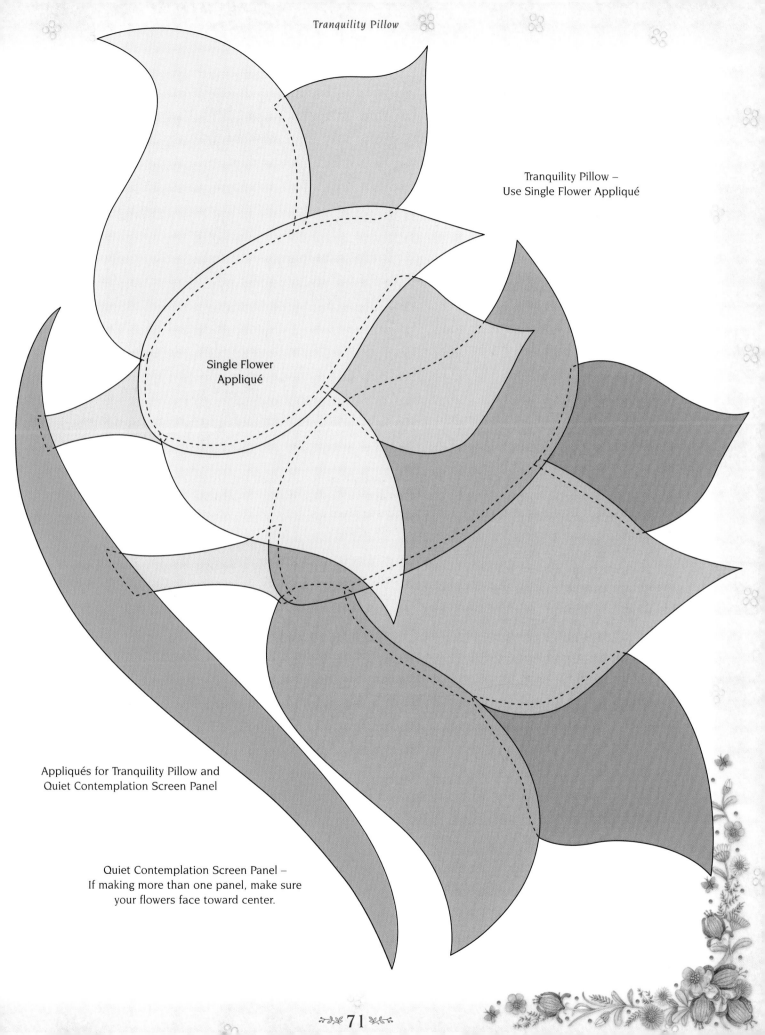

Tranquility Pillow –
Use Single Flower Appliqué

Single Flower
Appliqué

Appliqués for Tranquility Pillow and
Quiet Contemplation Screen Panel

Quiet Contemplation Screen Panel –
If making more than one panel, make sure
your flowers face toward center.

> "A garden is
> a place to feel
> the beauty
> of solitude."
>
> ~ Bob Barnes

# Quiet Contemplation
### Screen Panel

## Panels Have Many Uses

These lovely quilted panels can also be used as window treatments for French doors or stretched on rods–either singly or in groupings–for elegant wall décor. When teamed with the wood frames pictured on page 75, they can be purely decorative, or put to utilitarian use as well. Try them in multiples to disguise storage in a bed, bath, or family room, to create a dressing area or dramatic headboard in your boudoir, or to carve out a bit of home office space in a little-used nook or cranny.

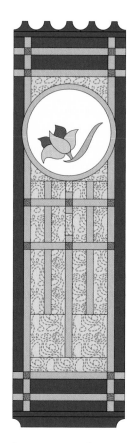

**Quiet Contemplation Screen Panel**
*Finished Size: 16" x 55"*
*Photo: page 75*

*Give your personal retreat a decorator touch with this tasteful and discreet quilted screen. Designed to complete our bedroom ensemble of the Tranquil Garden Bed Quilt (page 62) and Tranquility Pillow (page 68), this upscale accessory would be equally at home anywhere you want to foster a serene environment. Yardage and instructions are for one panel, but you can make as many panels as you wish.*

## Fabric Requirements and Cutting Instructions

Read all instructions before beginning and use 1/4"-wide seam allowances throughout. Read Cutting the Strips and Pieces on page 78 prior to cutting fabrics.

| | First Cut | | Second Cut | |
|---|---|---|---|---|
| *Fabric required for one panel* | Number of Strips or Pieces | Dimensions | Number of Pieces | Dimensions |
| Fabric A Borders and Tabs *5/8 yard* *Fabric must be 42" wide.* | 2 | 3 1/8" x 42" | 2 | 3 1/8" x 16 1/2" |
| | | | 10 | 3 1/8" x 3 1/2" |
| | 1 | 2 1/2" x 42" | 2 | 2 1/2" x 11 1/2" |
| | 4 | 2" x 42" | 2 | 2" x 41 1/2" |
| | | | 2 | 2" x 11 1/2" |
| | | | 4 | 2" x 2 1/2" |
| | | | 4 | 2" squares |
| | 1 | 1 1/4" x 42" | 2 | 1 1/4" x 16 1/2" |
| Fabric B Trellis/ Circle Border *3/4 yard* | 1 | 14" square | | |
| | 7 | 1 1/2" x 42" | 4 | 1 1/2" x 17 1/2" |
| | | | 1 | 1 1/2" x 15 1/2" |
| | | | 4 | 1 1/2" x 11 1/2" |
| | | | 2 | 1 1/2" x 9 1/2" |
| | | | 8 | 1 1/2" x 5 1/2" |
| | | | 2 | 1 1/2" x 3" |
| | | | 4 | 1 1/2" x 2 1/2" |
| | | | 12 | 1 1/2" x 2" |
| | | | 3 | 1 1/2" squares |
| Fabric C Accent Squares *1/8 yard* | 1 | 1 1/2" x 42" | 14 | 1 1/2" squares |
| Fabric D Background *3/4 yard* | 1 | 11 1/2" x 42" | 1 | 11 1/2" x 15" |
| | | | 1 | 11 1/2" x 2 1/2" |
| | 1 | 5 1/2" x 42" | 2 | 5 1/2" x 6 1/2" |
| | 2 | 2 1/2" x 42" | 4 | 2 1/2" x 9 1/2" |
| | | | 4 | 2 1/2" x 5 1/2" |
| | | | 4 | 2 1/2" x 3" |
| | 1 | 1 1/2" x 42" | 1 | 1 1/2" x 3 1/2" |
| | | | 1 | 1 1/2" x 2" |
| Fabric E Circle Appliqué Background *3/8 yard* | 1 | 12 1/2" square | | |
| Backing *1 5/8 yards* | 1 | 16 1/2" x 55 1/2" cut lengthwise *Remaining fabric can be used for a second panel.* | | |
| Appliqués (flowers, leaves, and stems) - assorted scraps<br>Batting - 21" x 60" | | | | |

## Constructing the Panel

**1.** Sew one 2" Fabric A square, one 1 1/2" x 2" Fabric B piece, one 2" x 2 1/2" Fabric A piece, and one 1 1/2" x 2" Fabric B piece in order shown. Press. Make four.

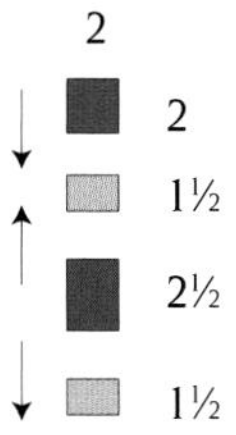

Make 4

**2.** Sew one 1 1/2" x 2" Fabric B piece, one 1 1/2" Fabric C square, one 1 1/2" x 2 1/2" Fabric B piece, and one 1 1/2" Fabric C square in order shown. Press. Make four.

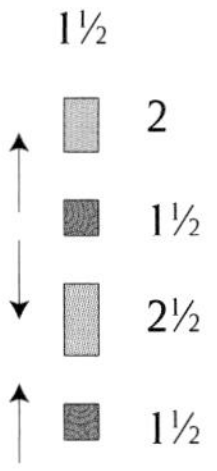

Make 4

**3.** Sew one 2" x 11 1/2" Fabric A piece, one 1 1/2" x 11 1/2" Fabric B piece, one 2 1/2" x 11 1/2" Fabric A piece, and one 1 1/2" x 11 1/2" Fabric B piece in order shown. Press. Make two.

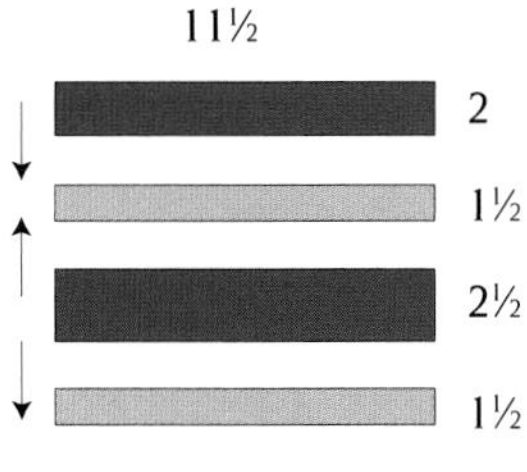

Make 2

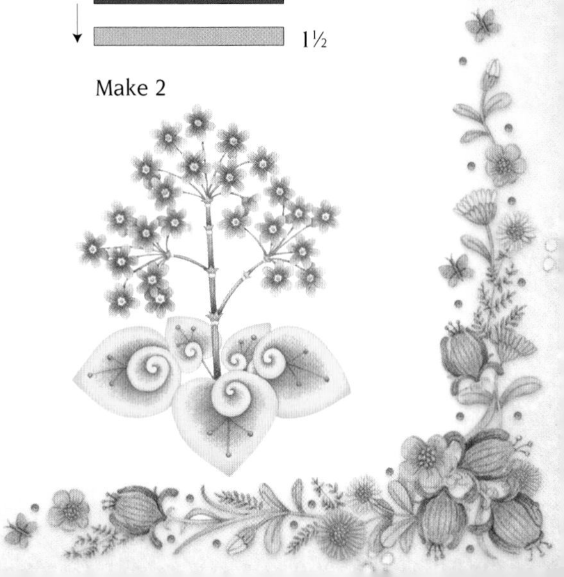

**4.** Sew one unit from step 1, one unit from step 2, one unit from step 3, one unit from step 2, and one unit from step 1 in order shown. Press. Make two.

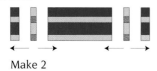

Make 2

**5.** Sew 1 1/2" x 2" Fabric D piece to 1 1/2" Fabric B square. Press.

1 1/2

2

1 1/2

**6.** Sew one 2 1/2" x 3" Fabric D piece, one 1 1/2" x 3" Fabric B piece, one 2 1/2" x 3" Fabric D piece, unit from step 5, one 2 1/2" x 3" Fabric D piece, one 1 1/2" x 3" Fabric B piece, and one 2 1/2" x 3" Fabric D piece in order shown. Press.

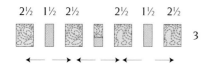

2½ 1½ 2½   2½ 1½ 2½

3

**7.** Sew 11 1/2" x 15" Fabric D panel to unit from step 6. Press.

11½

15

**8.** Sew unit from step 7 between two 1 1/2" x 17 1/2" Fabric B strips. Press.

1½     1½

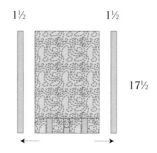

17½

**9.** Sew one 1 1/2" Fabric C square between two 1 1/2" x 5 1/2" Fabric B pieces. Press. Make two.

5½     1½     5½

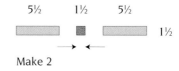

1½

Make 2

**10.** Sew one 1 1/2" x 3 1/2" Fabric D piece between two 1 1/2" Fabric B squares. Press.

1½

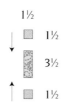

1½

3½

1½

**11.** Sew one 2 1/2" x 5 1/2" Fabric D piece, one 1 1/2" x 5 1/2" Fabric B piece, one 2 1/2" x 5 1/2" Fabric D piece, unit from step 10, one 2 1/2" x 5 1/2" Fabric D piece, one 1 1/2" x 5 1/2" Fabric B piece, and one 2 1/2" x 5 1/2" Fabric D piece in order shown. Press.

2½ 1½ 2½   2½ 1½ 2½

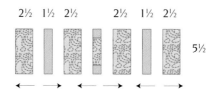

5½

**12.** Sew unit from step 11 between two units from step 9. Press.

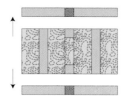

**13.** Sew 1 1/2" x 5 1/2" Fabric B piece between two 1 1/2" Fabric C squares. Press. Make two.

1½

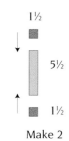

5½

1½

Make 2

**14.** Sew unit from step 12 between two units from step 13. Press.

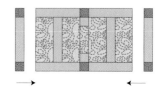

**15.** Sew 1 1/2" x 9 1/2" Fabric B piece between two 2 1/2" x 9 1/2" Fabric D pieces. Press. Make two.

2½  1½  2½

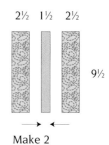

9½

Make 2

**16.** Sew each unit from step 15 to one 5 1/2" x 6 1/2" Fabric D piece. Press. Make two.

5½

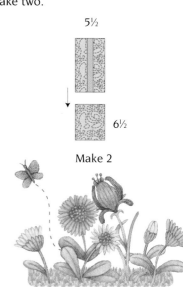

6½

Make 2

**17.** Sew 1½" x 15½" Fabric B strip between units from step 16. Press.

1½

15½

**18.** Sew unit from step 17 to 11½"" x 2½" Fabric D strip. Press.

11½

2½

**19.** Sew unit from step 18 between two 1½" x 17½" Fabric B strips. Press.

1½          1½

17½

**20.** Sew unit from step 8, unit from step 14, and unit from step 19 to make a vertical row as shown. Press.

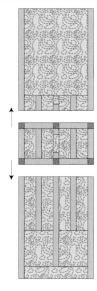

**21.** Sew unit from step 20 between two 2" x 41½" Fabric A strips. Press.

2          2

41½

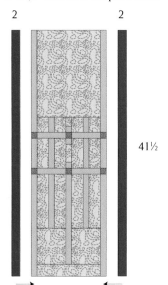

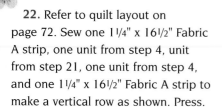

**22.** Refer to quilt layout on page 72. Sew one 1¼" x 16½" Fabric A strip, one unit from step 4, unit from step 21, one unit from step 4, and one 1¼" x 16½" Fabric A strip to make a vertical row as shown. Press.

## Preparing the Appliqué

Refer to Quick-Fuse Applique directions on page 78. If you prefer traditional hand appliqué, be sure to reverse all appliqué templates and add ¼"-wide seam allowances when cutting appliqué pieces. Refer to Hand Appliqué directions on page 79.

**1.** Fold 12½" Fabric E square vertically and horizontally into quarters to find center point. Trace appliqué pattern below for appliqué circle background. Cut out Fabric E circle appliqué background and refer to quilt layout on page 72 for placement. Position circle on panel with temporary fabric spray adhesive. Note that appliquéd circle border overlaps trellis border.

**2.** Secure circle to panel with machine straight stitch. To eliminate shadow, carefully trim away Fabric D background from behind Fabric E circle appliqué background, leaving ¼"-wide seam allowance.

**3.** Refer to Quick-Fuse Appliqué directions on page 78. Trace appliqué patterns on pages 71 for flowers and leaf.

**4.** Refer to quilt layout on page 72 and position appliqués on panel. Fuse appliqués in place and finish with decorative machine stitching as desired.

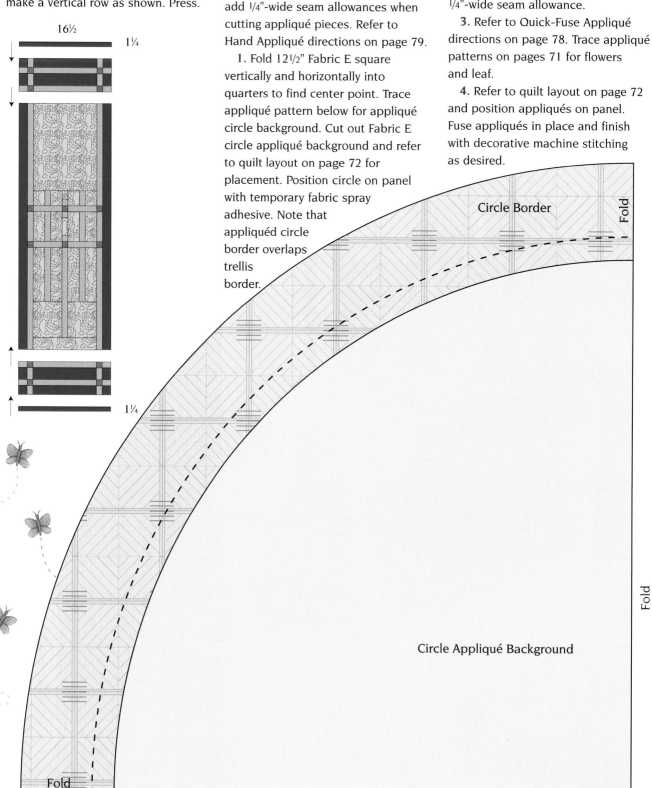

Circle Border

Fold

Fold

Circle Appliqué Background

Fold

Fold

## Layering and Finishing

**1.** Use tab pattern below to make template. Trace and cut one tab from each 3 1/8" x 3 1/2" Fabric A piece. Place tabs right sides together in pairs, and sew on curved edges as indicated on pattern. Clip curves if necessary and turn right side out. Press. Fold in half crosswise and press. Make five tabs.

**2.** Use tab pattern to trace curved edges on each end of one 3 1/8" x 16 1/2" Fabric A strips. Place the two strips right sides together and sew on curved edges as indicated on pattern. Clip curves if necessary and turn right side out. Press. Fold in half lengthwise. Press.

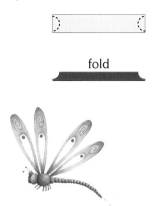

fold

**3.** With right sides together and straight raw edges aligned, space tabs from step 1 along top edge of panel. Stitch in place. Repeat to stitch sleeve from step 2 to bottom edge of panel.

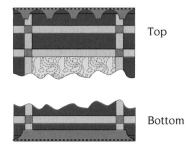

Top

Bottom

**4.** Keeping tabs folded toward center, as shown above, position top and 16 1/2" x 55 1/2" backing right sides together. Center both pieces on top of batting, and pin all three layers together. Using 1/4"-wide seams, sew around edges, leaving a 6" opening along top edge for turning.

**5.** Trim backing and batting to same size as top. Trim corners, turn right side out, and hand stitch opening closed. Press.

**6.** Hand or machine quilt as desired.

# QUIET CONTEMPLATION SCREEN WOOD FRAME

*Finished Size: 20" x 66"*
*Photo: page 75*
*These simple wooden frames are easy to construct and add dramatic impact to the quilted panels. Make as many as you wish and link them with piano hinges.*

**Materials Needed for One Frame**
*Two 16" lengths and two 66" lengths of 1" x 2" lumber*
*Two 17" lengths of 5/16" dowel*
*Tape measure, pencil*
*Wood glue and pegs and/or L brackets and screws*
*Sandpaper, paint or stain, & paintbrush*

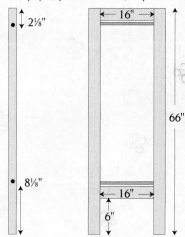

**1.** *Using 3/8" drill bit, drill holes 1/2" deep on one narrow edge of each 66" length of lumber as shown in diagram.*

**2.** *Refer to project layout and use two 16" lengths and two 66" lengths of 1" x 2" lumber to assemble frame. Fasten pieces together as indicated in layout using wood glue and pegs or using "L" brackets screwed to the back side. Be sure to square corners and use clamps to hold pieces together until glue is thoroughly dry.*

**3.** *Check to make sure 17" dowel fits in drilled holes. You may have to trim dowel down or sand lightly for a snug fit.*

**4.** *Lightly sand frame and dowels and paint or stain as desired.*

**5.** *Run one dowel through tabs at top of quilted panel, the other through sleeve at bottom. Insert dowels within top and bottom edges of frame, stretching quilted panel to fit snugly.*

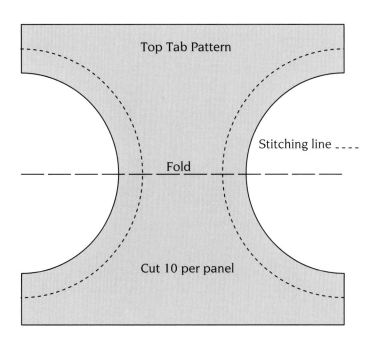

Top Tab Pattern

Stitching line - - - -

Fold

Cut 10 per panel

# GENERAL DIRECTIONS

## Cutting the Strips and Pieces

Before you make each of the projects in this book, pre-wash and press the fabrics. Using rotary cutter, see-through ruler, and cutting mat, cut the strips and pieces for the project. If indicated on the Cutting Chart, some will need to be cut again into smaller strips and pieces. The approximate width of the fabric is 42". Measurements for all pieces include 1/4"-wide seam allowance unless otherwise indicated. Press in the direction of the arrows.

## Assembly Line Method

Whenever possible, use the assembly line method. Position pieces right sides together and line up next to sewing machine. Stitch first unit together, then continue sewing others without breaking threads. When all units are sewn, clip threads to separate. Press in direction of arrows.

## Embroidery Stitch Guide

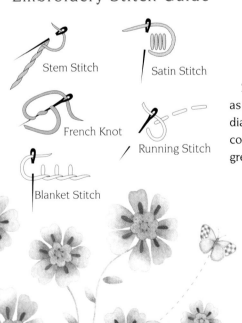

Stem Stitch

Satin Stitch

French Knot

Running Stitch

Blanket Stitch

## Quick Corner Triangles

Quick corner triangles are formed by simply sewing fabric squares to other squares or rectangles. The directions and diagrams with each project show you what size pieces to use and where to place squares on corresponding piece. Follow steps 1–3 below to make corner triangle units.

1. With pencil and ruler, draw diagonal line on wrong side of fabric square that will form the triangle. See Diagram A. This will be your sewing line.

A.

sewing line

2. With right sides together, place square on corresponding piece. Matching raw edges, pin in place and sew ON drawn line. Trim off excess fabric leaving 1/4" seam allowance as shown in Diagram B.

B.
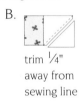
trim 1/4" away from sewing line

3. Press seam in direction of arrow as shown in step-by-step project diagram. Measure completed corner triangle unit to ensure greatest accuracy.

C.
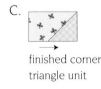
finished corner triangle unit

## Quick-Fuse Appliqué

Quick-fuse appliqué is a method of adhering appliqué pieces to a background with fusible web. For quick and easy results, simply quick-fuse appliqué pieces in place. Use sewable, lightweight fusible web for the projects in this book unless indicated otherwise. Finishing raw edges with stitching is desirable. Laundering is not recommended unless edges are finished.

1. With paper side up, lay fusible web over appliqué design. Leaving 1/2" space between pieces, trace all elements of design. Cut around traced pieces, approximately 1/4" outside traced line.

A. fusible web
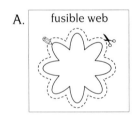

2. With paper side up, position and iron fusible web to wrong side of selected fabrics. Follow manufacturer's directions for iron temperature and fusing time. Cut out each piece on traced line.

B. fabric-wrong side
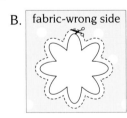

3. Remove paper backing from pieces. A thin film will remain on wrong side. Position and fuse all pieces of one appliqué design at a time onto background, referring to color photos for placement.

## Appliqué Pressing Sheet

An appliqué pressing sheet is very helpful when there are many small elements to apply using a quick-fuse appliqué technique. The pressing sheet allows small items to be bonded together before applying them to the background. The sheet is coated with a special material that prevents the fusible web from adhering permanently to the sheet.

**Directions:**

1. Prepare fabric for appliqué using your choice of fusible web.

2. Cut out each appliqué piece using pattern or template and remove paper backing.

3. Heat iron on low to medium setting. With a non-sewable fusible web set the iron on a lower setting. Let the fabric cool completely before lifting it from the appliqué sheet. If not cooled, the glue on these products could remain on the sheet instead of the fabric.

4. Lay the appliqué pattern on a work surface. Place the pressing sheet on top of the pattern and tape in place at each corner so that the sheet won't slide. The pattern should be visible through the pressing sheet. Lay the fabric pieces down one at a time as shown on the main pattern. Press to adhere to the pressing sheet, layering the appliqué design as you go. Let fabric cool completely. Pull up the design and the entire fusible web will still be on the fabric. The pressing sheet will not remove any of the bonding if used properly. If the design has several sections that are layered and then placed on top of other fabrics, you may layer and press these pieces together first. Pull up each section and lay them to the side until you are ready to lay the smaller sections on top of the larger piece of fabric.

5. Place the design on the fabric or item being appliquéd to, press in place and follow pattern instructions to finish the edges.

## Hand Appliqué

Hand appliqué is easy when you start out with the right supplies. Cotton or machine embroidery thread is easy to work with. Pick a color that matches the appliqué fabric as closely as possible. Use appliqué or silk pins for holding shapes in place, and a long, thin needle, such as a sharp, for stitching.

1. Make a template for every shape in the appliqué design. Use a dotted line to show where pieces overlap.

2. Place template on right side of appliqué fabric. Trace around template.

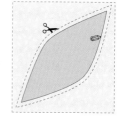

3. Cut out shapes 1/4" beyond traced line.

4. Position shapes on background fabric. For pieces that overlap, follow numbers on patterns. Pieces with lower numbers go underneath; pieces with higher numbers are layered on top. Pin shapes in place.

5. Stitch shapes in order following pattern numbers. Where shapes overlap, do not turn under and stitch edges of bottom pieces. Turn and stitch the edges of the piece on top.

6. Use the traced line as your turn-under guide. Entering from the wrong side of the appliqué shape, bring the needle up on the traced line. Using the tip of the needle, turn under the fabric along the traced line. Using blind stitch, stitch along the folded edge to join the appliqué shape to the background fabric. Turn under and stitch about 1/4" at a time.

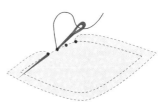

## Machine Appliqué

This technique should be used when you are planning to launder quick-fuse projects. Several different stitches can be used; small narrow zigzag stitch, satin stitch, blanket stitch, or another decorative machine stitch. Use an appliqué foot if your machine has one. Use a tear-away stabilizer or water-soluble stabilizer to obtain even stitches and help prevent puckering. Always practice first to adjust your machine settings.

1. Fuse all pieces following Quick-Fuse Appliqué directions.

2. Cut a piece of stabilizer large enough to extend beyond the area you are stitching. Pin to the wrong side of fabric.

3. Select thread to match appliqué.

4. Following the order that appliqués were positioned, stitch along the edges of each section. Anchor beginning and ending stitches by tying off or stitching in place two or three times.

5. Complete all stitching, then remove stabilizers.

## Adding the Borders

1. Measure quilt through the center from side to side. Trim two border strips to this measurement. Sew to top and bottom of quilt. Press toward border.

2. Measure quilt through the center from top to bottom, including the border added in step 1. Trim border strips to this measurement. Sew to sides and press. Repeat to add additional borders.

## Mitered Borders

1. Cut the border strips as indicated for each quilt.

2. Measure each side of the quilt and mark center with a pin. Fold each border unit crosswise to find its midpoint and mark with a pin. Using the side measurements, measure out from the midpoint and place a pin to show where the edges of the quilt will be.

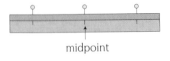

midpoint

3. Align a border unit to quilt. Pin at midpoints and pin-marked ends first, then along entire side, easing to fit if necessary.

4. Sew border to quilt, stopping and starting 1/4" from pinmarked end points. Repeat to sew all four border units to quilt.

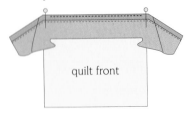

quilt front

5. Fold corner of quilt diagonally, right sides together, matching seams and borders. Place a long ruler along fold line extending across border. Draw a diagonal line across border from fold to edge of border. This is the stitching line. Starting at 1/4" mark, stitch on drawn line. Check for squareness, then trim excess. Press seam open.

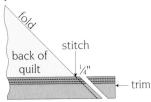

fold

back of quilt

stitch

1/4"

trim

## Layering the Quilt

1. Cut backing and batting 4" to 8" larger than quilt top.

2. Lay pressed backing on bottom (right side down), batting in middle, and pressed quilt top (right side up) on top. Make sure everything is centered and that backing and batting are flat. Backing and batting will extend beyond quilt top.

3. Begin basting in center and work toward outside edges. Baste vertically and horizontally, forming a 3"– 4" grid. Baste or pin completely around edge of quilt top. Quilt as desired. Remove basting.

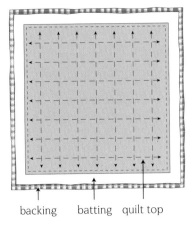

backing        batting   quilt top

## Binding the Quilt

1. Trim batting and backing to 1/4" from raw edge of quilt top.

2. Fold and press binding strips in half lengthwise with wrong sides together.

3. Lay binding strips on top and bottom edges of quilt top with raw edges of binding and quilt top aligned. Sew through all layers, 1/4" from quilt edge. Press binding away from quilt top. Trim excess length of binding.

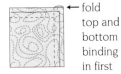

4. Sew remaining two binding strips to quilt sides. Press and trim excess length.

5. Folding top and bottom first, fold binding around to back then repeat with sides. Press and pin in position. Hand stitch binding in place.

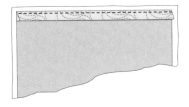

fold top and bottom binding in first

## Product Resource List

Debbie Mumm® products featured in this book were provided by the following companies:

**Ceramic Buttons** - Mill Hill/Gay Bowles Sales, Inc. (800) 356-9438, www.millhill.com

**Wallpaper** - Imperial Home Décor Group, (800) 539-5399, www.imp-wall.com

**Dinnerware and Collectible Teapots** - Sakura Inc./Oneida, Ltd., (212) 683-4000

**Stepping Stone, Plant Pics, and Flower Pots** - New Creative Enterprises, (800) 435-1000, www.ncegifts.com